Taught by pai

Mary Endersbee (Editor)
Valerie Hadert
Barbara Piller
Jack Wallace

FALCON BOOKS LONDON

First published 1970
Reprinted 1972

Mary Endersbee is Assistant Editor of *Crusade* magazine.

Biblical quotations unless otherwise stated are from the Authorised Version; the Revised Standard Version is copyrighted in 1946 and 1952

SBN 85491 523 0

FALCON BOOKS
Published by the Church Pastoral Aid Society,
Falcon Court, 32 Fleet Street, London EC4Y 1DB

Overseas agents
EMU Book Agencies Ltd,
511 Kent Street, Sidney, NSW, Australia

CSSM and Crusader Bookroom Society Ltd,
177 Manchester Street, Christchurch, New Zealand

Sunday School Centre Wholesale,
PO Box 3020, Cape Town, South Africa

Made and printed in Great Britain by
Billing & Sons Limited
Guildford and London

Preface

'I hope it's not going to be a depressing book,' a friend said, on hearing the title *Taught by Pain.*

To any who have doubts on the same score let me reassure you. The four contributors to this book write from a desire to tell how God showed them love, purpose, fruitfulness, even joy in their experience of pain, whether it was physical, emotional or mental.

It would be embarrassing to attempt an order of the contributions according to degrees or types of suffering, so I have arranged them (tactfully, I hope) according to age. If reading this book inspires you to trust God in the dark as well as the light, then writing it will have been well worth while.

TAUGHT BY PAIN

VALERIE HADERT comes from Romford and was a shorthand typist before illness forced her to give up work in her early twenties. She is now a permanent patient in a hospital in Brentwood but takes a lively interest in her local church and writes verse, some of which has been published in *Challenge* and *Decision*.

I

'It's no good, Val, I can't go on with it.'

John and I were sitting in the lounge at his home listening to Family Favourites on the radio. Elvis Presley's recording of 'Old Shep' was being played.

'What do you mean?' I asked, unsure what he was getting at.

'Look, I think it would be a good idea if you went upstairs and packed your case. There's a train due at any moment.'

I was spending the week-end at John's home the other side of London, about fifty miles from Romford where I lived. We had spent every week-end together for the previous two years, either at my home or at his. Yet, now he wanted me to pack up and go. I couldn't understand it. I was completely shocked. What was wrong? I tried to ask him and next minute he was on his knees with his head in my lap sobbing, 'Don't leave me.' What was I to do? Go, or stay?

In the end I went upstairs and packed my case. Then he saw me off at the station. And that was the last I saw of him from that day to this. His mother still writes to me even though this all happened ten years ago. He's married now with two children and I'm glad.

The hardest thing to take was not knowing why. The question haunted me: 'Why did John break it off? Why couldn't he go through with it?' It took five years for me to discover the full answer. And inevitably the thought of what is and what might have been has hit me at times, especially when what we called 'our tune', David Whitfield singing 'The Adoration Waltz', was played on the radio. Everything had revolved around him for two years and we had even talked about getting married.

I had met John through a friend at the youth club I belonged to. I was the energetic type, swimming three or four times a week, playing netball, and, at one stage, trying weight-lifting! Among other activities I joined the drama group at the club. A new girl there travelled, like I did, up to Liverpool Street by train each morning. We began to travel together and one day she asked me to make up a foursome with her and her boy-friend and his friend. Both lads were in the Navy. I'd never been on a blind date before but I agreed, and John was the fourth member of the party.

Before long we were 'going steady' and seeing a lot of each other. I was eighteen and life seemed marvellous. Then a strange thing happened. We'd planned to go to Clacton with my parents. That particular morning I woke up to find I could see *two* picture rails...and two of everything else! It was August, a few days after my nineteenth birthday and the double vision lasted for three weeks.

I was perfectly all right after that until the following Christmas when I found I was dragging a leg. This resulted in a visit to the London Hospital where the specialist advised complete bed-rest at home for a month, but by March I was unable to use my legs and had gone blind in one eye for a time.

Four months later, in July, John and I parted. I know he went through a great deal before doing so. He talked with my parents (who knew the cause of my symptoms) and went to his doctor. He asked him for advice about marrying someone with Multiple Sclerosis and was told that he would be a fool to consider doing so. The doctor told him some of the sordid details–and I've had experience of them too!

It was a fortnight before my twentieth birthday when he broke it off. I resumed my old life, trying to find other friends to fill the gap left by his going. I was very friendly with a girl down the road who had been born with double club feet. I didn't know the real reason for my various disabilities–General Neuritis was the name the doctors had used–and neither of us thought that I would be the one to end up in a wheel-chair. We used to go dancing together every Saturday night, but I couldn't forget John completely. The first boy who took me out arranged a trip to see *South Pacific* at the Dominion Cinema, Tottenham Court Road. When Rossana Brazzi sang 'This nearly was mine...one dream in my heart, one love to be living for, this nearly was mine', I just went to pieces. Everything hit me. I'd lost my health, I'd lost my job (through being off work with my illness) and I'd lost my young man. It seemed like the end of the world.

I can remember thinking through my misery, 'I'll ask Mr

Chase to pray for me.' Mr Chase was Superintendent of the Sunday School that I used to attend at the local chapel of Christian Brethren. I went one evening with every intention of speaking to him after the service, but I learnt that his wife was seriously ill. People said she was given only a few years to live, and I've heard since that she has had 'every removable part of her body removed'. I'm glad to say that she is still alive today, but at the time I felt Mr Chase's need was greater than mine and I didn't ask him to pray for me.

Nevertheless, the friendly atmosphere of the chapel so impressed me that I started going every Sunday. This meant that my week-ends consisted of dancing Saturday night and chapel on Sunday. Meanwhile I was working locally in a solicitor's office as a shorthand typist.

I'd taken commercial subjects at school and left with little ambition except to use my German. I didn't achieve this. Instead I became a typist, first in a solicitor's office then in export offices in London.

On Sunday nights a young lad from the chapel often gave me lifts home on the back of his Lambretta – he had a very understanding wife! My family had moved away from the chapel by this time, and I had to travel quite a distance. We've always lived in Romford as my father is a Green Line coach driver on the Brentwood–Aldgate and High Wycombe runs. This lad and I often chatted when he dropped me at my gate. We talked about life, and faith, and I sensed I didn't understand all that the folk at the chapel believed. They seemed to have an assurance I wanted and needed.

This situation got to such a pitch that I would sit through the service every Sunday, clutching my hankie and choked with tears. I knew the preacher was talking to me and about me. Finally one Saturday evening I prayed that *this* Sunday I would find someone older to talk things over with. The next day, after the evening service, the young lad said, 'Hey, there's a Squash on, are you going?'

'What's a Squash?'

'Oh you know. Five – or five hundred people – you all squash in! Are you coming?'

I said that I'd love to and we went. Halfway through the older man in charge, Mr Pettifer, stood up.

'Now, I know you younger folk would like to talk sometimes

with an older person about your problems, but you're afraid of attracting attention at the back of the chapel after the services. If there's anyone here tonight who'd like such a chat, just take my arm or Mr Mayers', and we'll be glad to talk with you.'

I managed to take Mr Mayers' arm and reach the back room, but no sooner did I get inside than I burst into tears. Somehow I gasped out my fears.

'I know I've accepted Jesus Christ but I don't feel any different; I hear the speakers talking about the "joy of salvation", but I don't feel any. It makes me wonder whether or not I'm really saved...'

Mr Mayers let me pour it all out, then assured me that if I had truly accepted Christ into my life, then the joy would come. He helped me to decide to make a fresh start. I rededicated my life to Jesus Christ–'reaccepted Him' if you like–and the joy *did* come. I know because it is still with me today.

A couple of months after my talk with Mr Mayers the chapel held a baptismal service. I felt it was an ideal time to be baptized, and to make it an even happier occasion Mr Mayers' daughter was among those baptized with me by her father.

That was 1960. I was twenty and working locally, but it was not long before a further setback occurred. I'd had my twenty-first birthday when suddenly I lost the use of a hand and arm. I could not take dictation so the firm I was working for put me on the switchboard. But before long I was in hospital. I faced this with a sense of dread as it was the first time since my conversion that I had been unable to share in the fellowship at the chapel, and I had come to depend so much on the help and encouragement of my Christian friends. I prayed that there would be another Christian in the ward so that we could have fellowship together.

Soon after I was admitted a lady patient came up to my bed, and, seeing my Bible, asked if I was a Christian. I told her that I was.

'Lovely!' she said, 'I've been praying for another Christian to come. It's the first time I've been away from home since I became a believer.' We were each the answer to the other's prayer.

Slowly my illness began to take on a pattern. It seemed as though I had bouts of symptoms every other year or so. The first when I was nineteen, then when I was twenty-one, then at twenty-three. Again, on my twenty-fifth birthday I was in hospital. I've had so many different symptoms at various times that I tend to lose track, but my twenty-fifth birthday I recall most distinctly, because it was the last time I can remember walking.

Three months before that birthday I had gone into hospital as a permanent patient, unable to leave my bed unless in a wheel chair. As a break from the London Hospital I was at the Convalescent Home at Banstead. Four friends came in their cars to take me out to tea to celebrate my birthday and we went to Box Hill. I had a wheel-chair, and they pushed me around in that. At one point they helped me out of the chair, and I walked a short way–only about ten yards, hanging grimly on to the arm of a friend.

It was about this time that I began to tackle the doctors about what was wrong with me. I wasn't wholly satisfied with 'General Neuritis', and one day a sister, in showing round a visiting doctor, said, 'This is Valerie with Multiple Sclerosis.'

Well, I was shaken rigid. I had met several people over the years in the hospital who had 'MS' pretty badly and but for them the name would have meant little to me. I was determined to know the worst–or the best.

When Sister had finished showing the doctor round I said to her, 'You told that doctor I'd got Multiple Sclerosis.'

'Well, what did your doctor at "The London" tell you that you had?'

'He said I'd got General Neuritis.'

'You can believe that then can't you?'

I thought about it and realized that, yes, I could–but I wasn't really satisfied. The end of my 'holiday' at the Convalescent Home was drawing to a close and when I got back to 'The London' I made my mind up to ask the doctor there. To add to my determination, a physiotherapist commented one day that my complaint had been on 'Dr Kildare' the night before. I soon found out that the complaint had been Multiple Sclerosis!

When I at last tackled the doctor I approached the subject carefully.

'Doctor, I've been told I've got General Neuritis, but I've been putting two and two together and I think I've got Multiple Sclerosis.'

He looked a little startled. 'What did Dr E...tell you?'

'He said I'd got General Neuritis...'

'Look, I haven't got time to talk to you about it now, but I'll have another word with you later.'

He came back after his lunch, obviously having prepared what to say. 'Look Valerie. Dr E...was right. You have got General Neuritis, but there is definitely an element of Sclerosis there.'

At last I knew, despite the indefinite way he had put it. And certainly the knowledge makes more sense of the various disabilities I've suffered during my illness. On several occasions I have lost the use of my legs and have had to lie on my back for weeks on end. Then for a time I was 'dead' from the neck down (and some might add 'from the neck up'!). I've nearly always had double vision. When I mention it to anyone I usually add, 'You're beautiful, dear...both of you!' That often makes them stop and smile.

I've also had a bout of deafness. I had always thought a deaf person could hear absolutely nothing. But if the noise I could hear in my head – like a loud vacuum cleaner – is anything to go by, I know that I'd have preferred to hear nothing!

Perhaps my worst time was when I was 'dead' from the neck down, my speech was slurred, I had blurred and double vision, total deafness and one side of my face had dropped! I knew I was looking odd, and this made me feel terrible when anyone came, mainly because it was a blow to my vanity. A girl can't help caring about her appearance, however ill she feels.

During the six years when I had 'MS' but didn't know it my family and several friends who knew the truth never so much as hinted that I had more than 'General Neuritis'. Looking back over those years, I can remember things I said or did that must have caused pain unwittingly, especially to my mother.

During one of my many stays in 'The London', I told her how sorry I felt for the middle-aged lady in the opposite bed.

'It's dreadful...she's got Disseminated Sclerosis. Do you know, she's had it since she was seventeen? Shame isn't it?'

Another time when my mother was helping me into the house, I couldn't manage to lift my foot on to the doorstep, and ended up on the ground. For some reason I got a fit of the giggles. Perhaps it was the thought of Mum, four foot eleven tall, struggling to get me, nearly five foot seven, to my feet. I felt dreadful when I suddenly realized that she was in tears.

But I shall never cease to be thankful for all that she has done for me. She doesn't enjoy good health herself, but she has been wonderful.

In January 1966 I came to the hospital where I am now. It is the Marillac Hospital at Brentwood, a home for the chronic sick run by Sisters of Charity, a Roman Catholic order. The Sisters are wonderful people. The hospital is very modern and light with three units of sixteen beds each: pink, blue and green. I am in the Pink unit in a ward of six beds.

I was 26 when I came to the Marillac, having been in the London Hospital since May 1964, about twenty months in all. 'The London' told me that the Marillac was for 'the young chronic sick' and took patients between the ages of 15–40. This was quite true, but unfortunately when I arrived I was the only one in that age range. (No, that's not strictly true – someone was 39½!) And since then hardly anyone has come in who is younger or as young as myself, so the past years have been lonely at times.

But my family and friends are very good. Besides my mother and father I have four brothers and four sisters and also seventeen nieces and nephews! One brother is in Australia and two of my sisters who are Christians are married to Christians. My younger brother has also professed Christianity.

My friends from the chapel come to take me to the morning service every Sunday, visit me regularly, and include me in any other activities they can. With the use of a sliding board and assisted by some willing helpers I can be lifted in and out of cars. The sliding board was the reason for one friend calling me 'Buttercup'. One day as he was trying to get the board underneath me he said, 'Come on – buttock up!' I've been 'Buttercup' ever since!

So with my helpful band of friends I have been able to attend several weddings and other 'dos'. One of my happiest outings was to a Wedding Shower held in a granary – the largest room they had available – which was reached by an almost vertical metal ladder. I had two fellows at the front, two at the back and one below who was shouting out encouraging remarks like, 'Don't worry if she falls, I'll catch her.'

Also I am very fortunate regarding visitors: I get quite a few.

In November 1966 I had to go into Harold Wood Hospital to have an ileal-bladder operation as the paralysis had left me incontinent. What could have been a miserable time proved a much happier one because members of St Peter's Church, Harold Wood, visited me. They came because a friend from chapel mentioned to them that I was in the hospital. We hit it off so well during my stay of eight weeks that they still visit me at the Marillac, coming every Tuesday, and I've got to know a lot of people at St Peter's through this.

But the reason for my stay in Harold Wood Hospital was not nearly so pleasant to remember. The operation was very nauseating and I was unable to keep any food down after it. When the surgeon came round the tenth day after the operation and saw me being violently sick he said, 'Theatre for you tonight, my girl.'

I thought for a moment he meant a seat to see *My Fair Lady,* but it wasn't. Back to the operating theatre I went to have the adhesions which were blocking my intestines severed.

These operations at the Harold Wood Hospital were the first I'd had since having my tonsils out at the age of five. I've certainly made up for that gap since, with eleven operations in the past three years!

The third of these was to straighten one of my legs which had become drawn up until I was literally kicking myself in the pants! I went into the London Annexe for it: a laminectomy which involved severing some nerves in my spine. After the 'op' I was unable to stir and I had five nurses to turn me every couple of hours: one at each leg and shoulder and one holding my head. It was one, two, three... heave... then the sharp agonizing pain zig-zagged up and down my spine for a few seconds and it was a case of one, two, three...and Valerie was in tears.

My tears I find very difficult at times. I am a very weepy person. I know it's a release, but I feel so annoyed with myself, especially when I let others make me weep. Here in the ward it's the worst. I find I clash head-on with some of the other patients, particularly on two scores. One is open windows and draughts. The other women are always hot and I'm a chilly mortal because my circulation isn't all it should be. Also I've been told by the Neurologist not to catch a chill on any account so draughts worry me. Then the TV gets me down because it's always so loud. I wouldn't be without its entertainment value but it is very noisy. 'How can you stand it?' asked a visitor one day.

'Well, to be quite honest, I can't. I just have to put up with it,' was all I could say. If I do complain on either of these points it creates a lot of ill feeling.

Sometimes I burst into tears for no reason at all. The doctor says that this is part and parcel of my illness, but I've been accused many times of wallowing in self-pity and crying because I can't get my own way. It's true that I have done so but only rarely.

When I cry I feel I am letting the Lord down and this worries me no end. I can picture people thinking, 'She calls herself a Christian, and just look at her!' This is particularly true when I get worked up (another thing I've been told to avoid!) in a person-to-person clash. I invariably end up in tears, in which case I'm accused of 'trying to get sympathy', whereas nothing could be further from the truth. In fact, I would give anything *not* to cry, as I feel my tears give the other person the upper hand and I like to stick up for my rights – although I know I shouldn't. I get an acute sense of injustice if the other person is 'top dog' when I think she is in the wrong.

The laminectomy should have left me unable to move my legs, but unfortunately it was only partially successful and my left leg still 'spasmed' and remained bent. I had a further operation on the back of my left knee to straighten the leg and, as my big toe was sticking up in the air and I didn't particularly want to hitch a lift anywhere, the tendon there was severed. One would have thought that was enough, but a few weeks later I found that my foot had dropped and I could not get a shoe on properly so my achilles tendon had to be elongated.

On top of this I have been back to Harold Wood Hospital twice since the big ileal-bladder operation: the first time for a cystectomy (total bladder removal); the second for the removal of a kidney stone, or at least that was what it should have been. I was first on the list that day and when I went down to theatre I had the surgeons mystified. The stone had disappeared. I didn't come out of the anaesthetic until five o'clock because they'd taken further X-rays on the operating table. It wasn't a waste of time because they found and dealt with the adhesions that had caused the elusive stone.

So my stay here at the Marillac has been interrupted at intervals over the years for visits to 'The London' for operations to my legs and spine, and to Harold Wood for the ones on, wait for it, my urinary tract!

2

I have tried to sketch in the past, and the ups and downs of my illness. Perhaps it is now time to look at the present and my life seen from a wheel-chair and a hospital bed.

Although I spend a good deal of my time in bed, I am up most mornings in a wheel-chair. The Marillac has its own chapel, like many other hospitals, but as it is Roman Catholic I don't attend the services. But as in most hospitals there is just nowhere to be on your own, so I go to the chapel to be quiet any morning I can. Sometimes when I am low because I've had a clash with one of the staff or patients, or I'm just feeling plain miserable I sit in the chapel and sob my heart out to the Lord. I don't know what I would do without Him.

But I can only stay up for about five hours in the wheel-chair because my back begins to ache. I think it's more because of the laminectomy than the sclerosis. I find the muscles on my left side pull which leaves me with a slightly twisted pelvis.

On Sundays when I am taken out by my family or friends, I usually stay in my wheel-chair for lunch and then sit in an arm-chair or a safari bed for the afternoon, with a pillow at my back. After morning service at chapel there are half a dozen or so homes to which I can go, including my own. This means there is a rota, and it is not too much for anyone.

Reflecting on the present makes me realize that though I have had eleven operations in three years I haven't had a sclerosis attack for five years, and that is great! I was having them every other year before and they were getting worse each time. At the moment I am unable to use my legs, and have double vision, but that's all that is wrong with me. It's wonderful! I put it down to the prayers of my friends. There are probably hundreds of people praying for me regularly and I believe that makes all the difference.

Of course, I'm fortunate in that Multiple Sclerosis is not a painful complaint. I feel pain if someone moves my legs too far. I suppose the muscles aren't used and have become 'set', but on the whole gross discomfort would describe what I feel.

But discomfort is not the only problem I face. I have mentioned the frictions over draughts and the noisy TV. Another real difficulty is one particular person who has never hit it off with me. She says things like, 'What a difference it would make if you were a Catholic...you wouldn't feel this way...you wouldn't say that or do this.' I feel I'm being belittled all the time. I'm not being criticized constructively but maliciously. Perhaps we clash because we are both on the forthright side, or too egocentric. Whatever it is I usually end up in tears. Those wretched tears. I know they are meant to be a safety valve. All I can say is I must have an over-active one!

On the other hand, through being in hospital, I have been able to find many real friends, and one advantage is being a Christian. Firstly there are the many friends among the patients and staff of the hospitals I've been in. In the London Hospital, where I spent twenty months, I always kept my Bible on my bedside table as I do now. Often someone would come up to chat and say, 'I see you have your Bible...' and before long I would find another Christian friend. And these friendships have lasted. Only last year when I went to stay with my sister in Norfolk it was a nurse who had cared for me three or four years previously in 'The London' who took me.

It is amazing how we ever met again because after I left the London Hospital we lost touch. She says she often wondered how I was getting on, then one day while reading *The Way I See It* by Cliff Richard, she came across a reference to 'Valerie Hadert in a hospital at Brentwood, Essex'. She immediately telephoned various Brentwood hospitals until she found which one I was in, then paid me a surprise visit.

On two other occasions I have been taken to stay with my sister by nurses from 'The London'. I got to know many people from the nurses' and students' Christian Union there, and among my friends are physiotherapists, sisters, occupational therapists and such like. We have got on famously because we are Christians. I firmly believe my list of friends would be more than halved had I not been a Christian or in hospital.

Then there is, of course, my crowd of friends from the chapel. When I went into the London Hospital in 1964 for the long twenty-month stay, my friends from Rise Park Chapel came by car every Sunday and Tuesday to see me. Often it was a car load, which meant six visitors altogether. In those months there were only two occasions when no one came, and this was because on one night the crowd were out singing, and on the other they had got in a muddle over the rota. They drew up a rota for visiting me. Isn't that great?

I laugh when I remember how I became a member of the singing group. They asked me to join and I said I'd got a dreadful voice.

'Can you make a good cup of tea?'

'Well, yes.'

'Right, you're in. We could do with someone like you to finish up the evening for us.'

But then a similar thing happened at my sister's church. When asked if she would like to join the church choir she said the same thing as I did, and the vicar patted her on the shoulder and said, 'Never mind, my dear. God made his crows as well as his canaries.'

Among my friends there are lots of children. Several of the couples at the chapel have young children, and they have been along to the hospital on several occasions to sing to us. I don't know who enjoys it more, the women or the children! Certainly the children are encouraged to come and the sisters always reward them with bottles of 'pop', biscuits and sweets.

Last year a group of children performed the pantomime *Cinderella* for us; all because of my verses! A friend from the chapel offered to type anything for me and as I'd written a dozen or so children's verses and knew about forty children under ten who might appreciate them if they were duplicated and put in a little book, I asked her to help. Subsequently a lady in her office took home a copy of the booklet as she had three children. The children enjoyed the verses so much that they asked if I would write some for the pantomime they were staging for their families and friends.

I agreed, on one condition: that they come to the Marillac and perform the pantomime for the ladies, which they did. We have a large recreation hall complete with stage, so they were able to use that. The youngest girl, the Fairy Queen, aged five, recited several of my verses, and said her favourite from my booklet was 'Tommy'.

Tommy next door has been naughty today,
So his Mummy has said he can't come out to play.
Poor Tommy!

It seems he was spanked and was sent up to bed.
But perhaps we could play games like 'I spy' instead?
'Hey Tommy!'

He came to the window, still wiping a tear.
'Would you like to play "I spy"?' 'Cor, that's an idea.'
Said Tommy.

The next fifteen minutes just seemed to fly by.
I really enjoyed myself playing 'I spy'
With Tommy.

Then his Mummy heard him and angrily said,
'I thought that I told you to get into bed,'
To Tommy.

Why, you should have heard Tommy's Mummy complain.
She smacked him and sent him to bed once again.
Poor Tommy.

My personal favourite is 'Oh Dear!'.

We wrestled on the grassy verge
Beside the flowers and
We wrestled by the roundabout
And wrestled in the sand.

We thoroughly enjoyed ourselves,
But when the day had gone
I suddenly remembered that
I'd got my best suit on!

And 'Santa's Christmas Present' comes a close second.

'What would you like for Christmas dear?'
They ask such silly things.

What would I like for Christmas?
Why whatever Santa brings!

He's bound to bring a train set
'Cos I wrote that in my note,
And I also asked if I could have
Some new sails for my boat.

I made my note sound so polite,
I know he'll bring as well
One of those big red buses with
A hooter and a bell.

I'd also like a puppet,
But I made sure that I said
If he couldn't get me all these things
A bike would do instead.

Maybe here I should explain about my verses. I have always written verse. I can remember writing it when I was ten, and I wrote the usual dubious doggerel about teachers at secondary school.

When I was courting, my verses became romantic love songs and after my conversion, I composed religious poetry. Not because I particularly wanted to, but it was just that the verses that came to me were along those lines. If I want to write serious poems now, I usually go to the chapel for some quiet. But before I was in hospital verses would come to mind in all sorts of situations.

Not long after my conversion I was on my way to church in dreadful weather. I had boarded the bus half-way through a thunder storm. When I got off I found it had stopped raining, and while the sky behind me was still black with storm clouds, ahead of me it was perfectly clear, and the sun was shining brightly. One line of verse flashed through my mind, 'The moistened roofs were glistening as they caught each dazzling ray'. Some weeks later I completed my first 'religious' verse.

The stormy air was stifling, and above the humid heat,
Darkened clouds of dull depression overhung the dismal street.
With angry, roaring voices they conspired to do their worst;

They groaned, they groused, they grumbled, and then, with a
sudden burst
Of anger that re-echoed loud, the rain began to fall
Relentlessly; it cleared the air; and then in due course, all
Their anger spent, the dreary clouds departed one by one,
And there before me I beheld the beauty of the sun:

The focal point of silver in a liquid lemon sky,
Shining through the dewy dampness of the rain. And I
Was conscious of a cool refreshing sparkle everywhere
As its bright beams were reflected by the raindrops in the air.
The moistened roofs were glistening as they caught each
dazzling ray,
And here and there a rippling pool of silver sunlight lay.

I stopped; and as I gazed entranced, it flashed across my mind
That the rolling clouds of thunder which were fading fast
behind
Could be likened to the misery and heartaches of today
When our Lord and Saviour cometh, for they, too, shall roll
away;
And as I pause, and muse awhile on all that He has done,
With wonder I shall gaze upon the beauty of the Son.

Eventually fourteen or fifteen poems were collected and put into a booklet called *From the Heart,* which was printed through the help of friends. Since then I have had a second booklet of verses printed and there are also the children's verses in duplicated form.

At the stage when there was just the booklet *From the Heart* printed, my sister, who is a Cliff Richard fan, wanted to give a copy to him. She told me that Cliff was converted and asked if she could take one of my booklets to give to him at the Palladium. She went off with the booklet and left it with his stage manager.

Several months after this I had a letter from a nurse I had known in the London Hospital, who was now a sister tutor. She had heard from a fellow sister tutor the rumour that Cliff Richard had been heard singing a song that had been written by me. I didn't think it could be true, so assumed they were imagining things.

But then the crowd from the chapel went to hear Cliff sing

in the Central Hall, Westminster, and he definitely was singing verses I'd written, and said so. A friend promptly wrote and asked him if there was any way by which I could hear him sing my verses, explaining I couldn't come to the meeting. He sent me a tape of his setting of my words which he has called *Think Again* and with the tape came a very nice letter.

Cliff has since sung this song all over the place, even in Tokyo! And he sang it in 1969 at the Royal Albert Hall, during the 'Help, Hope and Hallelujah' concerts. In November of that year the song was published in *Youth Praise 2*, the new youth songbook, and was sung on an LP record based on songs from the book.

In his letter Cliff encouraged me to send him any further verses I might write. So I send my efforts to him as and when inspiration comes. I often include some doggerel as well. Like this sort of thing:

Some verse I've heard is quite absurd,
Some dull and unexciting.
While other rhyme's a waste of time,
Like this piece that I'm writing!

It makes me want to add, 'How's your father?' 'All right!'

If I am to explain how I eventually met Cliff, I must mention my friends at St Peter's Church, Harold Wood. I've mentioned how I first met up with folk from that church when I was in hospital there, and they have visited me weekly since I came back to the Marillac. Also the 'Words of Life' singing group from St Peter's, who help with the hospital radio programmes, have been to sing to us.

Two friends at St Peter's, Fred and Robbie, knew about Cliff singing my song. On several occasions they had invited me to services at St Peter's but I hadn't gone. As I only get out once a week I like to spend the time with my friends from the chapel. However, over a year later shortly before Christmas, I was taken out on two consecutive Wednesdays and figured that going out for the day on Sunday might be overdoing things a bit. Perhaps it would be all right to go to St Peter's for just the morning service. When Fred and Robbie visited me on the Tuesday evening I asked if they could arrange for someone to take me there. They looked at each other significantly.

'Do you think we ought to tell her, Rob?' said Fred.

'Yes, or she'll only find out afterwards' said Robbie.

'Val, a friend of yours will be there in the evening.'

I'd heard rumours that Cliff might be coming sometime so I said, 'Not Cliff?' But of course, it was. So I went in the evening. Robbie wheeled me down to the second pew from the front so that I was only a few feet from Cliff as he sang and spoke. They also put a chair by me after the service so that we could have a chat. He seems a very nice chap with a wonderful sense of humour. A press photographer was hovering around and I looked up enquiringly.

'I'd like a photograph of you with Cliff if I may, please.'

'Hey!' I said to Cliff. 'He wants to take our photo.'

'Why? What's up?' said Cliff.

'I haven't combed my hair...'

He looked me up and down approvingly and said, 'You look...lovely!' I bet he says that to all the girls!

Another outcome of my meeting with Cliff has been the publication of 'my story' in *Challenge – The Good News Paper*. With the photograph of Cliff and myself at St Peter's to illustrate the article, I was able to share with the readers how I became a Christian, and how God has helped over the years. The Editor, Derek Sangster, having read my verses also suggested that I write a regular 'Val's Corner' for the paper. I've seen Patience Strong's 'corner' in one of the women's magazines and never thought that I would have the chance of writing one of my own. It means more than I can ever say to have such an opportunity to serve Christ from a hospital bed.

With my friends from St Peter's I was also able to go on their week-end conference in 1969 which was a great thrill. The week-end was made all the happier because a good friend called Keith loaned me his 'safari' bed. One summer when I had visited his home he had suggested I lie in the garden after lunch and produced this bed so that I could be in the sun with my feet up and a pillow at my back. When it was time to leave he said, 'Look Val, I'll keep the bed folded up in the boot of the car. If you want to borrow it at any time, just say the word and I'll bring it.'

So Keith kindly loaned me the bed to take to the Conference. I got up for breakfast, lay down in one of the downstairs rooms on the bed until lunch then I was up in my wheel-chair until after supper when I could lie down again without missing anything. I realized that without the bed I would have had to go upstairs to lie down and miss the fun. It would have been awful! The Lord provided for that need in His wonderful way.

I try to do a little in return for all that the St Peter's folk do for me. Robbie is editor of St Peter's magazine. As I'm watching TV or listening to the radio I keep my tissue box nearby and jot down the punch line of any good jokes I hear, then pass them on to him. (I have now collected nearly 200 jokes all neatly written on the tops of handkerchief boxes!)

My verses have come to me for varying reasons over the years. Sometimes I have been saddened by some incident, or at another I have been thrilled with the beauty of nature. Before long I find I can express how I feel best in verse. Take the time I was sitting on the veranda, marvelling at the spring. It was a beautiful day and I found myself lost in thankfulness and praise. What I wrote began:

O Lord, I thank you for the Spring,
When everything is new and gay;
For laughter, love, and each good thing
It pleases you to send my way;
For friendship, fellowship and fun;
For peaceful rest when day is done...

On another occasion there was a particular nurse, now a sister, in 'The London' with whom I was and still am very friendly. She told me that she no longer felt close to the Lord, and this so concerned me that I wrote some verses for her and handed her a copy. The last verse read:

But Thou art so gracious! Oh isn't it grand
Thy Word says no man can pluck her from Thy hand.
Didymus doubted and Peter denied
Yet both were drawn closer to Thy wounded side.
This, then, is my plea, may it not be in vain.
Dear Saviour, restore her first love once gain.

I was thrilled, when some weeks later she told me the prayer contained in those lines had been granted.

Then another verse, 'Wait on the Lord' was written about

battles of conscience. I wrote it over the course of weeks, as I do most of my verses. It remains one of my favourites probably because it reminds me of all that Jesus Christ went through for me and helps me realize more than anything else just how fortunate I am.

And if I am counting my blessings I mustn't forget the Sisters here at the Marillac. They are absolutely wonderful. Often they are short-staffed and I don't know how they keep going. Sister Mary in charge of my ward is great. I've had some good chats with her on religion. Once we discussed good works, and I said that it was only through the blood of Christ that we would get to heaven.

Sister Mary said, 'I know a man who says "I just can't accept it all". He's a very good man. Do you mean that on the last day God will say to him, "Hello Joe. Yes, I know you've been a good chap and done a lot of good things, but you can't come in here."?'

'Quite honestly, Sister, I think the Bible says yes, that really is what will happen. It says that many will say "Have we not done this and that and the other, Lord?" and God will say, "Depart from me for I know you not." If the man can't accept Christ on earth, then Jesus Christ won't accept him in heaven.'

At this she just looked at me and said, 'Well, Valerie, all I can say is, I'm glad you're not God!'

Sister Mary also has a great sense of humour and often has a laugh with us in the ward. She really is one of us.

I'm sure that my sense of humour has helped me when things might have become too much. We've often had a good laugh in the various hospitals I've been in. I think the funniest incident I remember was when I was in the London Annexe. All the patients were seated at the lunch-table as nurse wheeled in the food trolley.

'A choice today, ladies! Steak and kidney pie or fish. What would you like, Mrs Smith?'

'Fish please, nurse.'

Nurse served the fish then went on to the next patient.

'What about you Mrs Jones?'

Mrs Jones was looking out of the window day-dreaming; we all knew about what!

'Mrs Jones?'

'Oh...yes nurse?'

'What are you going to have, dear?'

'Oh, a hysterectomy.'

For all the laughs I get my gloomier moments. Cliff said in a letter that he didn't for one minute believe that I need cheering up. But I do. I feel very much left out of life, especially when I look at my friends. They're all married and have children, and this hits pretty deeply. They try to include me as much as possible in their family life. I stay the night with them perhaps, and one friend has even said, 'Don't worry about not having any kids, Valerie, you can share mine.'

Also I feel cut off from life as it happens in the big, wide world. Mind you there are advantages! At the time of the 1967 Middle East crisis, all my brothers and male friends were eligible for call-up so I was dreading a full-scale war. But during all the speculation I was in 'The London' for the laminectomy and by the time I was able to sit up and take notice everyone was talking about 'the six-day war'. Not only were my brothers and friends safe, but I had been spared the anxiety that everyone else had been through at the time.

Yet though, in a sense, my illness has cut me off from normal life, it also led me to the Lord, and through Him my verses have been used tremendously. This is fantastic, and I do not feel nearly as useless and helpless as I might.

And knowing the Lord makes my complaint easier to bear for I know I have a wonderful future. I know I could be ill at any time: next week, next month, next year. It's the prospect of my wonderful future in heaven that helps me to face it.

It is also glaringly obvious to me that I have an amazing collection of friends, though I'm in touch with very few friends I knew before I became a Christian. But look at my many Christian friends from all sorts of backgrounds: Baptist, Church of England, Pentecostal and Brethren! There's a great oneness, a unity and love between us all. Yes, I've got so much to be thankful for.

When I compare all my blessings with the things that are wrong, the blessings far outweigh the petty clashes and the other things. I don't know what I would do without the Lord. I've certainly been far happier the last ten years with Multiple Sclerosis than I ever was, healthy and strong, before I knew Him.

Perhaps one of my poems may sum up what I'm trying to say better than I can. It is called 'From a Wheel-chair'.

The scenes are changing
And the faces, too—
It's all a part of life's great plan—
Inevitable, unavoidable!
But oh! to have to sit and watch
And silently look on...
To feel that time is racing on
And leaving me behind...
Further...further...
Ever further behind.

Where is the merry crowd
With whom I spent
So many happy hours?
They are still here,
Still merry, jolly, gay;
But oh! transition!
They have their husbands.
Their children,
Their wives,
While I look on,
Silently watching...
Envying this happiness
That is denied me–
Longing...yearning...hoping!

And yet I have so much
For which to thank the Lord:
Family, shelter, care
And praying friends,
A helping hand when needed,
And a silent Listener
Who bends a sympathetic ear
To all my tales of trouble
And of woe.

I'm happy and contented
With my lot
Until I brood
Upon the things I lack
Instead of the abundance

Of all that I possess...
Begone, foul brooding!
Welcome, sweet content!
Pay no attention to those passing things
That came...and went!

MARY ENDERSBEE comes from Cheshire and worked in a bank before going to Bible College. She is now Assistant Editor of *Crusade* magazine.

B

I

The jangle of the telephone disturbed the Monday lunch-hour torpor. I glanced at my watch as I answered.

'Good afternoon. *Crusade* magazine.'

'Er–can I speak to–er–Mary Endersbee?'

'Speaking.'

There was silence. I waited with a growing suspicion that something was wrong. Nothing happened, yet the caller had not put down the receiver.

'This is Mary Endersbee speaking. Can I help you?'

A slight sound at the other end of the line encouraged me to try again.

'Did you want my help in some way? Is it...' I paused, then took the plunge. 'Is it something I've written perhaps?'

'Yes, it is.' A tearful voice said hesitantly. 'You see, I've been ill recently and in hospital for a nervous breakdown. And', the woman gulped and tried to stifle the quaver in her voice. 'I've been back at work a few weeks. Then last Saturday afternoon, this lady from the church I used to go to came round and she went for me. She said...she said...'

There was another long pause while she struggled with her tears. My own feelings were in a turmoil. I knew what she had been told. No one had said it to me until well after my breakdown but it still made me wince.

'Did she say a Christian shouldn't have a nervous breakdown?' I asked gently.

'Yes, she went for me. I asked her not to–to discuss it, but she would go on...'

I listened while she poured out the sad story, growing more and more angry with the thoughtless cruelty of the unwelcome visitor, and the lonely misery of my mystery caller.

'...she said I lacked faith. I just couldn't face going to work today, I'm in such a state...There's no one I can turn to who understands what it's like. Then I remembered seeing an article by you in *Crusade* magazine, and I felt, perhaps you would understand...'

Tears of sympathy and indignation stood in my eyes as I swallowed hard and tried to frame my answer.

'You know, as well as I know, that what your visitor said isn't true. When I had my breakdown I lost my faith, but God held on to me. I know that though I failed him He was faithful in His care for me. Mental illness is no worse than a physical illness in the sight of God. He hasn't let you go.'

By the end of the half hour conversation she had calmed down considerably and we were able to talk quietly about her illness and its causes, one of which was an unhappy marriage. I assured her that I would talk to a friend of mine who was a psychiatrist and send her any books I could find to help. I also assured her that if she felt the same sense of desperation again she could ring me. When I eventually put the phone down I was unable to hold back all the pent-up emotion her call had aroused in me. I sat and wept over her lonely agony caused by such a misguided sense of duty and a complete lack of thought.

But when I was calmer I was glad that I had been able to help. I was thankful that I had stayed in the office for my lunch and been there when the phone rang. I was also thankful to God for the experience that had enabled me to sympathize with her.

Four years previously I was anything but thankful.

It was the greyness I remember most. Drab grey winter days, the clouds unbroken by the faintest trace of winter sunshine, hung overhead like chill, colourless slabs of concrete. The view from my room in the hospital didn't help either. We seemed to be occupying part of a derelict Army camp, composed of wooden huts. Concrete slabs and stretches of grass separated the huts, and plots of soil showed evidence of cultivation.

I used to stand at the window watching for my mother's arrival to take me out. The first time I stood there and watched for her it was my second day in the psychiatric unit. I was adamant. I was not going to stay in what I had discovered was part of a big local mental hospital. I hated the place and the people. That morning the shock of finding the name of the big hospital on the linen and cutlery had forced me to ring my mother in desperation and beg her to come and take me away.

'But look darling,' she protested when she duly arrived with my suitcase that afternoon. 'You know as well as I do that you're not normally like this. You aren't well.'

'I'm perfectly all right.' I claimed through the wretched tears that wouldn't stop. 'I'm physically fit. There's nothing wrong with me really.'

'You're not usually weepy like this for a start, or depressed.' My mother persisted. 'I can't help you, only the doctors and nurses here can. What's the point of coming home, when they can do what I can't? You know you're not yourself...'

And inwardly, with a grim sense of finality I had to admit she was right. Three weeks before when I'd arrived home from training college, I had been completely and utterly finished. Christmas had failed to light the dampened fuse of my usually sensitive and lively spirit. Parties, presents, people and plans for my future had sunk into the greyness of my sense of depression and failure.

All through that autumn term at teacher training college I'd felt unhappy and unsure. I'd enjoyed doing a degree course at Bible college. The challenge of my finals had kept me going even when the sudden death of my father the previous autumn had broken into my academic cocoon. But at the training college doing a post-graduate course I found nothing to get my teeth into. The course demanded very little and I could make of it what I liked. On top of that I was lonely, not knowing many students at the college, and doing a course taken by relatively few people. All this meant I had too much time to think and brood. Before long I began to lose my appetite–an unheard of occurrence–and my sleep. Very early every morning I would awake with such a start that going to sleep again was impossible. Then like some ghoulish troupe of performers, my fears and worries seemed to rise up and prance through my mind prinking and parading every ghastly detail of the mess I was in, for my torment. It was a relief to get up and dress.

Then end of term teaching practice drew nearer and that only increased my tensions. This was my second attempt to do a teacher's training course, and I had given up before teaching practice on my previous attempt. This time I must stick it out. So the last three weeks of term found me grimly surviving a pretty gruelling daily bus journey to and from a huge comprehensive school. The staff were friendly but very busy. Somehow

I got through what I was set to do, although I have little idea what it was I actually taught. I remember odd scenes, the staff room noisy and impersonal, though filled with people; one of the school dining halls; drawing on the blackboard a map of the Holy Land and a sketch of Jacob; playing 'Downtown' and 'Mary's Boy Child' on my accordion. Certainly all my efforts seemed pretty futile to me, though no member of staff ever confirmed this impression.

Suddenly it was all over. I was home to what should have been a happy, relaxed Christmas, when I could come to terms with my unhappiness.

But the depression that settled on me was more than just a passing period of tiredness or unhappiness over my dislike of teaching. It gripped me like a vice. My mind could see nothing but ghastly failure, and for the second time! I could not bring myself to give up teaching, or to face up to the future and the finding of some other job. I talked endlessly, threshing about for the escape route that wasn't there. My poor mother was at a loss to know what to do with me. I was constantly in tears and when I wasn't I sank into a melancholy state or began to talk again. The suggestion that we go to the doctor made sense because I felt strange. I assumed I would be put on a course of tablets. Instead he advised a visit to the out-patients' clinic of a local hospital to see a psychiatrist. By this stage I was so sunk in gloom that making the decision to go into the psychiatric unit made little impression on me.

We drove the twenty-odd miles to the hospital on a typical grey chilly January day. The Sister, a tall, older woman with a kind smile, had made every effort to brighten the appearance of the day ward I was in. It comprised several corridors and rooms, and with gay curtains, carpets and potted plants in attractive holders the effect was quite colourful. I had a room of my own, a privilege I fully appreciated as most of the patients slept in two larger wards. There were two sitting-rooms for the patients of our ward, but we had our three main meals in a communal dining-room, at the other end of the hospital. With little appetite for food, and less for the diet they put me on at first, I did not enjoy mealtimes very much. It was one of the few occasions when patients from different wards saw each other, and I viewed the other people with suspicion, watching for the first signs of madness or violence to make themselves apparent.

I cannot remember making any friends in particular in my ward, but feel quite sure this was because I was too depressed to make the effort. I can remember lots of people who came and went during my two month's stay. Most of them were women older than me and most were married. I had half-expected them to behave oddly: scream, tear their hair, do all the things that mad people are supposed to do, but I know that all of them behaved perfectly normally and, like me, had their good and bad days. We were all on occasions weepy, morose, hysterical, talkative, nervous or just dopey from drugs or shock treatment. Though we were a very mixed bunch I saw nothing to substantiate the wild ideas about the mentally sick that I'd heard.

Of the few youngsters in the ward I remember one in particular for she seemed tragically restless and unhappy. With a friend she insisted on having the radio on 'constant pop' full blast while they chain smoked and jigged around. During my stay she ran away and had to be taken to the big hospital of which our unit was part. I heard she had also tried to take her life on several occasions.

After the fateful second day when I decided to stay, the hospital routine began to take over. Each morning we trouped off with a nurse to breakfast at the other end of the building. I glanced fearfully into other wards and at people we passed expecting the worst. When we arrived back at the ward we received our drugs and did some cleaning. I viewed my task as the last of many straws–I had to sweep out the toilets!

Occupational Therapy came next, and we were sent across to another building for this. 'OT' was done in what appeared to be a dark and cavernous hut. Patients could try their hand at a fair selection of crafts, guided and encouraged by a therapist. I don't recollect producing much of value and the one object I brought home, a half finished rug, has never been completed.

Breaks for coffee, and then lunch, were the main items on the timetable. But 'OT' was carried on until tea time when we returned to the ward. Supper in the dining-room followed later after which we could sit in the sitting-rooms unless we preferred to go to bed.

Two facilities for the patients that I sampled on a few occasions were the library, not a brilliant selection of books but then I couldn't concentrate anyway; and a self-service canteen where we could buy papers, sweets and refreshments. There was also a room with the label 'Industrial Therapy' but we never used this, and I assume it was for the men patients.

In my first week I was given a thorough medical check-up and I visited the Clinical Psychologist. Neither test produced any startling results, and regular talks with the psychiatrist became the main interruptions in my weekly routine. The basic difference in my daily timetable was my mother's visits in the afternoon instead of later. Because it was winter and the weather bad, the hospital agreed she could visit me then in preference to having to drive in the dark.

If my memory of the treatment I received is correct – and I'm told electro convulsive therapy tends to confuse the memory – I wasn't very communicative at the beginning of my stay in the psychiatric unit. I was too deeply engrossed with my own anguish. I didn't want to talk to the psychiatrist and I could not grasp what was wrong with me or why it was so. The blow to which I attached the greatest significance was my failure to teach. How could I have made such a ghastly mistake for the second time? Where had I gone astray? Why had God allowed it?

Perhaps because I was just not releasing all the inner tensions, I was eventually given a dose of LSD. I was kept in bed for this, and I remember a doctor or nurse hovering nearby with pen and paper in case I said something worth recording. But for a long time I lay silent, just feeling very strange. I saw unusual colours and my hands appeared to be twice their normal size. Then a few leading questions were put to me and my father came into the conversation. Suddenly the floodgates gave way. I cried as I have never cried before or since. I broke my heart because my father never lived to see me get my degree, a thing I knew would have made him inordinately proud and happy.

After that my father's part in my unhappiness became clearer and some unpalatable facts had to be faced. His death was a key factor in the whole maelstrom and perhaps this impinged the most upon my faith. My last visit to my father in hospital the night he died, the shock of seeing death written on his face, my inability to say any of the right things to him knowing that he had never shown interest in Christian things: this is the crunch for me. And it will be for a very long time.

However, one psychiatrist seemed to consider my worries about heaven and hell all part of my 'religious fanaticism' and therefore unhelpful. But it was not just the spiritual question marks I had to contend with when I thought of my father, there were the unpleasant memories of his part in my unsettled childhood. I had chosen to forget the many ghastly rows and my fear of my father's violent temper.

Although some of the repressed tensions were now battling their way to the surface I was still morose and very listless. I convinced myself in my blackest moments that I was destined to have the dreaded 'ECT' or 'shock treatment'. And I was right, but the course of treatment was not prescribed until my illness reached a crisis point one week-end. We were allowed home every week-end and it was unfortunate that on this occasion a college friend was staying and saw me at my worst. Months later, on seeing me again, she greeted me with, 'Thank goodness, you're smiling.' On the Sunday when we prepared to see her off at the station I expressed my fear that I might be tempted to throw myself under a train. Incredible as it seems to me now, I felt just like ending it all then. Without delay my mother whipped me back to the hospital and before long I was in bed and the decision made for me to have ECT.

Twice a week we were taken to another ward, anaesthetized and given the therapy. It left one with a blinding headache and usually unable to do much for the rest of the day. It also seemed to wipe the memory clean of the events of the previous day or so. But after three or four treatments the depression began to lift. I found I could respond to people. The world began to penetrate the strange fog I had been surrounded by over the previous weeks.

By my sixth week in hospital, the improvement continuing, I hoped very much that the psychiatrist would decide I didn't need the last two of the six prescribed treatments. I loathed the waiting, listening as the other patients were given their treatments before me, dreading the approach of the anaesthetist and the needle. But no, I was to have the complete treatment, and then see. The psychiatrist hoped I would be well enough to leave the unit a week after the final dose if, and it was an important if, I could find a part-time job.

I was beginning to take stock now. The past was a closed chapter that I had got to learn to live with. I had made the decision to give up the education course during my time in the hospital and had driven with my mother to fetch my belongings. It was a case of facing up to the present and future now, and that was to be a slow, and painful process.

2

During the last two weeks of my eight-week stay in the psychiatric unit I began to come to grips with myself. Before long I found the shock of having a breakdown at all was unpleasant enough to live with, without the hurtful facts about its cause adding to my dismay.

My faith was under fire the most in those weeks. Here I was, a Christian for nearly twelve years, Bible college trained, with a background in Crusaders, school Christian union and beach missions: taught that 'to worry was not to trust'; singing about 'peace perfect peace' and yet – it didn't work. My faith had not been strong enough to keep me at peace. I had failed God. My high ideals had crumbled about my ears. I was a useless spiritual wreck.

Each week-end at home I had made myself go to church on Sunday mornings but it had been meaningless. A numb leaden object had replaced my usually sensitive spirit, and previously well-known and well-loved hymns or Bible truths failed to touch me, or made me weep from a sense of self-pity. I had taken a Bible into hospital but it sat in my locker. The few attempts at reading it failed to help as I could not concentrate easily and little of the meaning of the words reached me.

Restless and sleepless at night despite heavy drugs, I would find the lonely sense of desolation that darkness brought almost unbearable. 'Oh God!' was the nearest I could get to prayer, wanting to add, 'Why have you forsaken me?' but not able to go on. My mind was unable to tackle abstract thought, so spiritual concepts failed to penetrate. My conscience, however, was unduly active and played havoc with me, telling me that I ought to make more effort to pray, or that God had forsaken me because I had failed to do His will. A misplaced sense of guilt was my daily and nightly companion.

And, well, just having a breakdown was a terrible blow to my pride. I'd always considered myself not the type, and had felt sorry for those who were troubled by their nerves. And here I was in a mental hospital – the place we'd always referred to as the 'loony bin' at school – with the threat of permanent mental disability hanging over me. For I felt so odd that I believed I would never be normal again.

It is hard to express adequately the weird agony of mental torment that racked me like physical pain at the time. It is the complete lack of normality that shakes you. My mind was in a turmoil and my feelings deadened so that I felt that I had gone mad and would never recover fully. I dreaded becoming a person who was considered a bit 'mental' or odd.

On occasions I visited the hospital chapel, a quiet empty room where a few of us took communion. The Anglican chaplain came to visit me and we talked about God's faithfulness. But another chaplain who visited me distressed me by implying that the Bible's authority was in doubt. I was in no fit state to argue with him and I was disappointed that what should have been a helpful visit was actually unhelpful.

Besides my mother and an aunt I had two other visitors from outside the hospital during the eight weeks. My mother drove the forty miles alone each week-day except when a neighbour came on one occasion. Buried beneath my own miseries I could barely stop to contemplate how my mother was standing the strain of my illness, but I sensed she was fighting a lonely battle. Few people understood what we were going through and I wish she could have had more support.

As it was, a friend asked a pastor of a local healing home to call on me. He arrived the afternoon our neighbour had accompanied my mother and I was in bed at the crisis point of my illness. I was not in the mood for talking and there was little to be said, but he did pray for me and I am grateful for that. When he left my mother accompanied him to his car and was shaken to be given the impression that unless I was removed from the satanic influence of the psychiatrists and the hospital there was little hope for me! To be told that when she could see how ill I was, yet not know what was for the best...Fortunately I did not know about all this at the time but I wish he had lessened instead of increased her burden.

During the week-days all that was home and church seemed very far away. Of visits from Christian friends I had none, but I invariably saw some of them at the week-end. A few letters and cards came but I could not face replying to them as I had nothing to say.

As the weeks went by and the first green shoots began to push through the frozen soil in the bare patches outside my window I sensed the depression lifting and a shred of faith thrusting feebly through in much the same way. I could not frame my thoughts into prayers but neither could I say 'There is no God'. But as God's presence gradually became a spiritual reality so did the gnawing question, 'Why did He let it happen?' For many months, this question remained unanswered and today I still feel I know only part of the solution.

But life had to go on. Although I knew I was by no means myself again I had to get accustomed to the idea of leaving the hospital. Though I had disliked it intensely at first I was very reluctant to go! For one thing it offered a sort of security, something known, while outside I had to find a part-time job and meet people.

The part-time job was offered to me by friends and I know it was a God-send. I washed up in the large modern kitchens of a local boys' boarding school. I found a warm welcome from my friends on the teaching staff and a ready acceptance among the domestic staff. Despite feeling very peculiar at times, as I was still taking a number of drugs, I gradually gained confidence and some of my fears of being thought 'queer' were quelled, especially as I was treated as normal.

The future I found more daunting. It was all very well dealing with the past but I had to look ahead for something more permanent to do. I was tempted to despair when I tried to think of what I could do, and often fell back into a veritable 'slough of despond'. This is the disconcerting thing about recovering from a breakdown. You make progress in a very slow, vague and unsatisfactory way. Not having had a breakdown before and knowing no one whom I could ask I often despaired as I sank back into a depression, or failed to sleep. I could produce irrational, imaginary worries to order at any time and must have bored my mother and my friends to tears with problems that bore little relation to reality.

Of course there were the routine check-up visits to the psychiatrist which helped to clarify some problems, but I was made to realize any dependence on the doctor was out of the question, and 'self help' was advisable.

Through my illness and the weeks that followed my mother was a tower of strength. Often at home when I could not sleep I would get up and find her still awake with her Bible open. I could just sit and weep away the tensions or talk through my latest 'worry'. Without her help my recovery would have been slower and less sure.

Then there was the fellowship of my friends at church. Here the habits of attending the services and meetings that I had formed over the years were a blessing. It is easy to run away from people and meetings when you feel weird, but force of habit often took me to a meeting, with little anticipation and enjoyment, yet I came away with a sense of Christian love and friendship surrounding me.

That Easter came and went with little impact. Usually the resurrection triumph meant a great deal but this year it was unable to touch me. I remember only how I loathed the Easter holidays when the school where I worked was empty and I could not keep up the job. So deadened had my spirit become that I could find nothing to interest me. Sitting in front of the television in the evenings only seemed to emphasize my dullness. Music, my greatest interest, had lost all appeal and I scarcely touched my gramophone or piano for months. Before, I usually played both daily.

Whitsuntide was approaching and our annual Christian convention with it. I had been persuaded by my friends from church to go but I remember it for one reason only I'm afraid: the bottle of peppermint flavoured medicine I took with me. It was the first of several useless bottles of medicine I was to see in the weeks ahead. The trouble was a strange abdominal pain I had developed. The doctor naturally put it down to 'nerves' and so prescribed quantities of peppermint mixture which duly disappeared, but the pains didn't.

I couldn't believe that within what seemed a few weeks of leaving mental hospital I was going to be ill again, but as May and June went by the pains got worse. I was still working at the school but trying hard to find a permanent job. I looked in the 'sits. vac.' column of the local evening paper and wrote off for interviews. But no one wanted me. With a theological degree and a nervous breakdown to my credit perhaps it was understandable.

My already low spirits sank lower. What else could I do?

Well, I'd done four years banking before going to Bible college. So, although it made my Bible training seem like a waste of time, I made polite enquiries about re-entering banking. I was on the point of filling in application forms when the blow fell. My pains were caused by gall stones and an operation was essential as soon as possible. The pendulum had swung from acute mental agony to acute physical agony within the space of six months, and I was ready to throw in the sponge. My efforts at job-hunting were finished. I was right back where I started. God who had already seen fit to lay me low with one blow had set me back on my feet only to knock me down again. It sounds crude, but that's how it felt!

On top of this I was scared stiff of the operation. I'd had enough of needles and hospitals to last me a lifetime and neither were the painful after-effects of the operation anything to look forward to. But uppermost in my list of fears was the dread of 'cracking-up' and having another breakdown.

In the end, apart from a few tears when I first went into hospital I settled down fairly quickly. The waiting for the 'op' was the worst: I kept imagining the surgeon's knife doing its job. Then afterwards I was so concerned with not being sick or moving about too quickly that the worst was over before I knew it. Gradually I improved and was soon up and chatting with the other patients. In the face of many reminders of human pain and death most had a cheerful courage. One older woman was an exception. She was terrified of the fairly serious operation she faced. I tried once to comfort her by talking about God's goodness, for I knew she was a Roman Catholic. She agreed with me but remained afraid.

Two events shook me out of my self-preoccupation. After an emergency case had been rushed into a bed farther down the ward, I looked over and recognized, with a shock, the bruised features of our next-door neighbour. She had been involved in a car accident, but fortunately was not seriously injured. Then during my second week a woman died in a side ward and seeing the gathering of bereaved relatives at her door brought back painful memories of my father's death.

But to brighten my stay my visiting hours were full of variety. All my friends rallied around and made a great fuss so that I had visitors every day and flowers and gifts galore. It was a strange contrast to my previous stay in hospital.

So all my worries proved groundless. Not that my stay had been exactly pleasant but I had been able to cope. And this proved to me in a more concrete way than any spoken assurance that I was 'on the mend' mentally. Post-operative depression, and the shocks I've already mentioned, caused moments of misery but I did not crack up.

Leaving hospital I faced convalescence with mixed feelings. I needed the rest but I also desperately needed a job. I gave myself a fortnight before I started job-hunting again. I hated not having a proper job and it was now eight months since I had first fallen ill. There was something soul-destroying about being unemployed. I lost my self-respect, and felt useless and unwanted. Added to which, my mother could not support me on a widow's pension and National Assistance wouldn't last for ever.

By this stage I had given up the idea of going back into banking. It seemed as if God had said 'no' to that when He put me back in hospital. But I tried for other jobs in Liverpool. One in particular offered very good training in computer programming, with excellent salary and prospects. I had to attend a day-length session for tests and interviews. I arrived home very tired and dispirited as I had not been one of the three chosen. The next morning opening *The Life of Faith* I read with a genuine sense of loss of the sudden death of Dr Ernest Kevan, my Principal at Bible College. My thoughts moved to London and before long I was writing off to Christian publishing houses for jobs. I had a vague desire to 'get into' something to do with literature and publishing.

To cut a long and miraculous story short I found a job, *the* job, at the end of October. The post hadn't been advertised; I just rang up and enquired about a job at the very moment when the need to fill a vacancy occurred. I came away from the interview walking on air! Someone wanted me. To boost my morale even more, before I received the official written offer of this job from London, I had a telephone call from Liverpool offering me one of the 'plum' jobs I had tried so hard for. I feel so thankful that I went into Christian work, not as a last resort – the only thing I could do – but out of choice, able to give up consciously the comfort of living at home and the good pay and prospects of the other job. Within a fortnight I had begun work and was living, as I thought temporarily, in a mews flat in Central London.

I was still not fully recovered from the traumas of the previous nine months! Leaving my mother alone up north to come to London wasn't easy for a start. We had become very close during my illness and I had come to depend on her constant encouragement. Then, I was taking sleeping tablets at night, and worrying myself sick if I didn't sleep. On top of this my spirits still tended to do a kind of see-saw from high to low at the slightest setback, and I kept a bottle of tranquillizers in my drawer in case of need. To put it mildly I was frantically worried about myself the whole time!

After some months, I think it was early in 1966, my supply of pills began to dwindle. I worked myself up into a great state about this. For one thing I wasn't registered with a doctor in London, and wondered if any doctor would understand the ins and outs of my nervous breakdown. When I eventually registered with a Christian doctor to have my prescription renewed he pointed out that it was a year since I had left mental hospital and didn't I think two sleeping tablets a night too strong?

Well, I did, but I was terrified to stop taking them. I firmly believed I could not sleep without them. His compromise solution was to renew the prescription but to suggest that I tried taking two on alternate nights. So I tried this and found that I slept quite well without the pills. I never took them again, and felt so much better in every way that I wished I'd stopped taking them sooner.

3

Looking back over the past five years to my breakdown I see it as a crisis-point in my life. Before it I know I was emotionally and spiritually immature, holding to a narrow set of ideals without due consideration for others. It is not that I think I'm now perfect...it's just that I seemed to 'grow up overnight' through the grim weeks of illness and uselessness. I lost some of the petty narrow ideals I'd set myself and others as I realized that true freedom of faith in Christ didn't depend on obeying a set of rules. My family say I became 'softer, less ready to judge'... and I am ashamed.

The five years have had their difficult moments. I discovered that I had less emotional resources to cope with 'problem' people than I thought. An alcoholic, for instance, whom my flat mates and I tried to help, reduced me to a tearful wreck and plunged me into depression. I felt desperately guilty that I never wanted to see her again and couldn't help her. But in the end I had to recognize that I couldn't cope with her and this 'weakness' was something I had to live with.

Depression when it does come occasionally (as it does to most people!) is in my case, usually brief, intense and associated with memories of my father's death. Time does not seem to have healed some of the deepest wounds and I have to accept this. But I must not give the impression that my life is a grim succession of depressions. I have never felt better! In fact, I feel humbled by God's goodness to me when I meet others not so fortunate. I know several people who have had several breakdowns when I have had one. Others have been ill for far longer and taken years to recover fully. And still others live with a permanent mental weakness that makes them psychological cripples.

Though I know I would rather go through the gall bladder operation again than have another breakdown, I can see that my experience of mental illness was not in vain. Naturally, for a start I have learned to treat the whole subject of mental health with a new respect. My wild ideas about 'loony bins' and the mentally sick have been drastically revised, and it has been a great help to talk things through with a Christian friend who is a psychiatrist. Not only can I understand a little better the reasons for certain methods of treatment but I also feel I understand my illness and its causes a little better.

This raises the question of Christians and psychiatry. I have met several people who, though not prepared to say that a Christian should not have a breakdown, still feel a Christian should not be treated by a non-Christian psychiatrist. As there is a shortage of Christians in psychiatry this creates obvious problems! I can only speak from my own experience. I was under two psychiatrists, neither of whom made any claim to be a Christian. One was clearly in disagreement with my religious convictions, the other took a more neutral position. Nevertheless I regained my health and my faith was restored the stronger for the whole experience.

In the end I think the trouble lies within the patient, not within the treatment. I don't believe a non-Christian psychiatrist is going to set out to 'destroy a patient's faith'. It is more likely that the breakdown or illness will do that anyway. No, the testing of my breakdown was the testing of the strength of God's grip on me and my hold on Him. If my faith had been more feeble or misplaced in a shallow, frothy Christianity instead of the sure Word of God I think my recovery would have made a different story, whether I had a Christian psychiatrist or not.

Then I was on 'drugs' for over a year: tranquillizers and sleeping tablets by the bottle. Again I have heard some Christians say a Christian should not need to take drugs. Was I failing God then? Only if I also believe that Christians should never have breakdowns and that I cannot accept. A breakdown is an illness with causes and symptoms like any other illness. If the doctor prescribes aspirin for influenza and I take those, then why should I not take tranquillizers and sleeping tablets to relieve the symptoms of mental illness?

So where some would look only for the harmful effects of psychiatry and drugs I can see only blessing and fruitfulness.

The breakdown has given me a foundation deep within my spiritual experience that is unshakeable, tested as the onslaught of the illness stormed at the defences of my faith and tore away my immature, untested ideas whittling my experience of God down to its basics. I look back and claim the promise of John 10 that no one can snatch me from His hand. No experience can be worse than the agony of that breakdown, I can face the future secure in His grip.

Perhaps the greatest joy God has given me through that experience is the ability and sympathy to reach out to others, especially those who have suffered or are suffering mental illness. It is very hard for anyone who has not experienced it to understand what it is like. (That sounds trite but unfortunately it's true!) I have lost count of the people who have shared with me their experience of mental illness, grateful to find someone who understands what it means. I cannot advise but I can sympathize! As with the lady who rang me at the office, this costs something, but it makes those months of pain and torment worthwhile.

Coupled with this are the opportunities God has given for me to write and speak on a subject about which most people feel they prefer to keep silent. I found myself woefully ignorant about the basic facts of mental health even after two months in a psychiatric unit. Naturally when I felt better I wanted to know why this and why that? Reading books has helped, and, of course, talking with other people who know more about the subject. In this connection, it is encouraging that more and more ministers and church members are taking courses in 'clinical theology', recognizing that so many of the pastoral problems in the Church today stem from psychological causes. But I'm afraid that in the Christian world there is still a tremendous stigma attached to mental illness – especially depression and what is commonly called a 'nervous breakdown'.

I say 'commonly called' because the term 'nervous breakdown' is the most familiar term used by the non-medical person for this form of mental illness. And whatever we call it there is still a fear of it, maybe because it is something unknown and strange to the majority of us. Surely the churches could help to enlighten those who think all mental illness means madness in the bad old-fashioned sense that I did. Nervous breakdowns are becoming so common today among Christians that it would help everyone if the subject was readily discussed and talked about. A little less ignorance and a little more sympathy would go a long way.

So in a way I am making a plea for extra concern to be

shown for any who suffer mental illness. 'Do you know, I never realized you would have liked visitors?' one friend said to me, sincerely surprised by what I wrote about my lack of visitors in the psychiatric unit. I think that person voiced the doubts of many who think mental illness is something very private – something to keep within the family. I think many also feel diffident about visiting a mental hospital and wonder exactly what's in store. Will the sick friend want to see them? In a general hospital you can usually be sure of a welcome, but in a mental hospital it can be heartbreaking to sense the visit has been apparently a burden.

The fact is that a deeply depressed person, for example, doesn't respond warmly to visitors. They just don't respond to anyone but herein lies the paradox. The patient wants to be reassured that there is nothing wrong with them (for they feel so strange) yet they long to be made a fuss of (for they feel so ill)! So though you may get little thanks for it, do visit friends who are mentally ill. Don't heighten their sense of horror at what has happened to them by cutting yourselves off from them.

The Mental Health Act 1959 recommends that the 'treatment of mentally ill patients should be provided with no more legal formality or social or geographical isolation than that involved in the treatment of any other illness' (*Psychiatry Today* by David Stafford Clark, Pelican). In other words the old, shut-away approach to treating the mentally sick is out. The National Health Service is seeking to treat as many as possible in our general hospitals. When I told my psychiatrist friend the hospital I'd been in allowed me to discover I was in part of the big, dreaded, mental hospital, I was surprised to find she thought this was normal and right. Remembering my shock at that time I found it hard to see her point. But she stressed how important it was to realize that a nervous breakdown was one of many forms of mental illness. And seeing the need now to remove the 'stigma' of mental illness and help mentally ill patients to see their sickness as just another 'illness', I understand what she meant.

As Christians we have tended to compartmentalize mental illness more than most. We've shut it away as something outside a Christian's experience – which is nonsense – and we have given Christians who suffer mental illness a terrible sense of inferiority and guilt. It is sad that Evangelicals who were in the forefront of so many works of compassion and social justice a century ago, are dragging their feet here. Mental sickness is no worse or different from physical sickness. (If I've said it too often, forgive me!) We have to accept that the Fall has disrupted the whole of nature: body, mind, spirit; and we cannot pretend one part is immune to illness just because we're Christians. Let's recognize, as our doctors and psychiatrists have done, that sickness in whatever form demands our concern and sympathy, and spare those who face mental illness unnecessary anguish.

Unnecessary anguish? Well, I may be sticking my neck out here, but I have in mind some who believe in faith healing. I see their motives are sincere, but I wonder if they realize how much of a burden they lay on a mentally sick person when they imply that they 'lack faith' or, to take it a stage further, that they are 'demon possessed'. I am not exaggerating for that was said to a friend during her illness. If there is comfort to be given surely it is better to pray for the sick friend than to tell them that sickness is the result of sin?

Taught by pain? Yes, taught that God has purposes in and through suffering. Taught, too, that mental illness is not the failure of faith but the testing of it and, more wonderful still, that if our faith fails, God does not let go of us, for when we are faithless He remains faithful.

BARBARA PILLER (formerly Mrs Barbara Clayton) comes from Manchester and is a trained nurse. After missionary training she went out to Rwanda with the Church Missionary Society in April 1960.

Nearly three years later she married John Clayton in Africa, and within a year found herself a widow and a mother.

I

It happened in the middle of Brahms' Violin Concerto. John and I were listening to it in the living-room of our bungalow at Buye, a small mission centre in Central Africa.

Three masked men burst into the room; two with spears and one with a sten-gun. At first I thought it was a joke, but as I think back, I remember that I was soon practically paralysed with fear as the sten-gun seemed to be levelled at me.

The men were speaking in a language I couldn't understand but recognized as Swahili. John tried to get through to them by speaking French.

It was all so bizarre. They were threatening and speaking in a language that made no sense, the record player was still filling the room with Brahm's music, John was obviously trying to reason with them and I seemed frozen to the settee feeling helpless and full of panic.

Of course I knew what they had come for. There was a small safe in our bedroom and John kept all the College money there. A few weeks earlier when I had been away at the Sister's house to have our baby, there had been an attempt to break into the safe, and an earlier attempt before that. Now they had come back – armed to the teeth.

John was standing just in front of me and for some reason he was holding a cushion. Perhaps the intruders thought that he had a gun behind it. I shall never know. What I do remember clearly is that he made a fairly sudden movement when he turned to speak to me, and that's when it happened.

The man with the sten-gun fired at us both. The room was full of explosion and smoke. And John fell.

He simply said 'They've shot me!' and blood began to pour – I thought – from his left arm. This galvanized me out of my panic. I rushed towards the men, literally pushed them out of the door and ran towards the doctor's house. I remember feeling that it was miles away but all the time I consoled myself desperately with the thought that John had only a flesh wound.

I was wrong. When James Derrick, the doctor, and I got back to the bungalow we found that John had a bullet through each lung. He died about an hour later. He was unconscious and there was nothing we could do.

Of course, the death of a husband is bound to bring shock and grief to anyone. But for me the pain was especially hard to bear. We had faced obstacle after obstacle that seemed designed to prevent our marriage taking place in the first place. We had been married for fractionally less than a year and our first child was barely two weeks old. As a missionary nurse I had accepted the prospect of spinsterhood only to fall in love, marry–and on that March evening to become a widow.

Some people's love stories are dramatic; some are perhaps tempestuous; some romantic in the true novelettish manner. But falling in love for me was just thoroughly inconvenient! It had happened when I was spending my last few days at home before setting off for my first tour of duty in Africa with the Ruanda Mission. I had been nursing for nine years and during my time at a Salvation Army Hospital I had been convinced that God wanted me to serve overseas. I can't pretend that I had jumped at the idea but I nevertheless became more and more convinced about it and finally began missionary training in Chislehurst in 1958. Courses in Tropical Medicine in Liverpool, and then in Belgium (where I also tried to learn French) had followed. In the spring of 1960 I was due to sail.

That takes me to Easter 1960–a time that I shall never forget.

My home is Manchester, I was born there, my parents lived there; and for that matter, they still do. My 'home church' was Holy Trinity Platt–a large, fairly imposing neo-Gothic building with a congregation of warm-hearted people. I had much to do during my last three weeks before embarkation.

On the first Sunday morning back in Manchester, I went along to church and heard John Clayton, the curate, preach. It was the first time I had ever set eyes on him. I can't pretend there was anything particularly special about him, his sermon or my reactions, except that he looked rather ill. But then he was the pale, somewhat gaunt type, and was just recovering from 'flu.

We met in the porch afterwards and he spoke of his own hopes for missionary service. He seemed anxious to talk more–to compare notes, so we met at his digs later in the week.

It wasn't long before he had invited me to join him and another girl, who was also preparing for missionary service, on a picnic and walk in Lyme Park some twelve miles away. I remember thinking it was a bit odd of a young curate to take not one, but two girls out for what he called 'a day of fellowship together', but I went.

I remember also another feeling during that carefree day. I found I slightly resented the fact that I didn't have John to myself!

Then came Good Friday and the communion service. As ever, when I was home, I found myself helping out in the choir. This meant that I was stationed in the choir stalls opposite the curate as he stood at the communion table and clearly in his line of vision. During the reading of the epistle, John looked up from the book. Our eyes met and I suddenly knew I was in love with him. It came like a blinding flash just as the magazine romances say it does. But unlike the magazines and pop songs – the realization brought me no joy whatsoever.

That night I wept in my room, praying that John and I could fall out of love just as clearly as we had fallen 'in'. I remember feeling that God was somehow unfair to have let this happen. There was I with most of my belongings on their way to the boat for East Africa. And there was John with at least two more years in England ahead of him and ambitions to serve God in the Moslem world. To fall in love was the cruellest thing that could have happened to us both.

Easter Sunday's evening service was also a sort of parish 'valedictory' for me. At one point during the service I was expected to speak. But my thoughts were confused. I suppose I sounded all right but I must confess that my mind was far from the mission field.

The crunch came on the Tuesday after Easter. We met just before midday in Platt Fields, the local park. It was one of those bright, cold April days that reminds you that winter is still not far away. John told me that he also had 'fallen in love'. We sat down on a park bench within sight of the vicarage and prayed. At the time we seemed amazingly matter-of-fact about it. We could see no prospect of any meeting, let alone marriage, in the near future. I was about to sail for East Africa and John felt called to the Middle East. We just prayed there in the crisp coldness that God would bring us together in the future if that indeed was His will.

And that was it! John took me to the bus at 12.30, shook hands and saw me aboard. I muttered something about flying home via Jerusalem and the bus pulled away. John stood there watching until he was a small figure in the distance and blurred by my tears.

I remember the conductor kept asking 'Sure you're all right, luv?'

I sailed for Africa on the *Kenya Castle,* quite prepared to face a future without John, but I cannot pretend that I was free from self-pity. Arrival in Africa helped me greatly. There were so many new impressions to fill my mind and so many new people to meet. The journey from Mombasa to Bujumbura in Burundi was a particularly memorable event. We went via Nairobi and Kampala. Groups of African Christians met us at the various railway stations. Their energetic pumping of our hands and the warmth of their greeting of 'Tukutendereza' ('Praise the Lord') did much to cheer my spirits. There is a radiance about an African Christian which is quite indescribable.

My first post in Africa was to be a sister in the mission hospital at Kigeme in Rwanda. I arrived there in November 1960 after completing a course in tropical medicine at a Government hospital in Bujumbura. During my time at Bujumbura we were dealing with thousands of refugees fleeing as a result of the political upheavals in the newly independent Congo. Some of them advised me, as a white person, to go home. They probably didn't realize that, for other reasons, I wanted to do just that!

When I arrived at Kigeme I found more refugees there also. This time the trouble was a civil war between the two main tribes in Rwanda. I can still remember the sight of African huts on fire.

But all this suffering and trouble did serve at least to keep me busy, and looking back I would say that my time at Kigeme was one of the most fulfilling periods in my brief missionary experience. The hospital was busy: there were nurses and male hospital dressers to train, we had a building programme on our hands, and there were always opportunities to talk to people simply and naturally about Christ.

In fact, I was beginning to escape from my self-pity and my thoughts of John. Then one day I received a letter from him. We had agreed, back in Platt Fields on that chilly spring morning, that there was little point in writing but John had found a reason. He was teaching in his local school and the children wanted to adopt a missionary. John wrote to ask if I would be willing to co-operate–and so began our correspondence.

Things, politically, were getting worse in Rwanda. I was transferred to a hospital in Buye in Burundi and no sooner had I arrived there than I found myself in the middle of what had become for me a familiar situation–refugees. This was September 1961, and thousands were streaming across the border from Rwanda to the comparative safety of Burundi. Soon every available building was filled to capacity and my memories are full of slithering around in red mud trying to cope with a dysentery epidemic. Everywhere I looked there were cold, wet, hungry people. Many were sick. We were short of medicines. Many died.

John was, by then, writing regularly. His link with the children was finished as he had started training at the Church Missionary Society training college in Chislehurst. In 1962 he wrote to tell me where he was being sent. It was to the Moslems of Sudan–not to the Middle East. This was great news for me. He was only going to be 1,000 miles away, and in African terms that seemed just around the corner!

However, things didn't work out quite so smoothly for John. He began to realize that getting a visa to enter Sudan might take a long time.

One morning at Buye the principal of the nearby theological college, Alan Lindsay, visited the hospital. He had obviously a load of problems on his mind. He told us of the desperate need for another ordained man on the College staff. He wanted a man who could speak and teach in French and who had completed missionary training. His plan to offer some highly educated young Africans an advanced theological course to prepare them for ordination seemed to be in jeopardy.

As I heard him talking I thought of John kicking his heels in England waiting for his entry permit into the Sudan. He fitted the bill exactly. I mentioned his name and Alan Lindsay jumped at the possibility. To the amazement of us all, arrangements with London went through smoothly and John was all set to fly out to join us in Buye in January 1963.

And when January came–I took ill.

It was decided that I should take the first lift going to Uganda that was available. In Uganda I could get treatment and take some holiday. Lifts were infrequent, but only two days after the decision was made a car that could take me to Kampala was due to leave. With many regrets I packed and left Buye. I hadn't had a letter from John about his arrival details but it seemed certain that he would come via Bujumbura – 500 miles from where I would be.

It was a depressing journey to Kampala which took several days. Eventually I arrived in the outskirts of the town, and looked for somewhere to telephone the CMS Guest House and book in for the following day. A familiar voice answered on the other end of the line. It was John – he had arrived a few hours earlier.

I shall never forget that first evening in Kampala. I had arranged to meet John after supper but the supper where I was staying for the first evening, was somewhat of a farce. I was almost ill with excitement and couldn't eat a thing. As I was driven into the city to meet John I kept trying to remember what he looked like – it had been nearly three years and we had only seen each other over a period of a few days. Meeting him again was one of those wonderful moments that only seem trite in words so I shall not attempt a description.

The next day I moved into the CMS Guest House as previously arranged and that evening John proposed. The sudden acceleration of events lent a dream-like quality to everything – I couldn't bring myself to believe it was actually happening to me. We bought the ring and the days passed with us moving around in a sort of rose-coloured mist. As far as I am concerned, Kampala, and particularly Namirembe Hill, will always have a sort of magical air about it.

Realities, however, have to be faced and the return journey to Buye had to be made. It is true that John was with me but there were difficulties in our new relationship. We did not announce the engagement and I did not wear the ring. The weeks passed at Buye with both John and I finding it hard to concentrate on our respective jobs in the college and hospital. We had to exercise great restraint in order not to offend the conventions of the local people. It seemed to us as if we were back in Victorian England.

Then came the moment I dreaded. John heard that his visa had come through. He was clear to go to the Sudan in April.

We announced our engagement on March 30th, and on April 1st we said goodbye.

I had hoped that the separation would not be too long and we talked of meeting up with each other when I was due for some leave in July or August. My health however dictated otherwise and that summer the Mission decided to fly me home to England for treatment. It was doubly vexing, but more was to follow. No sooner had I arrived in England than I received news that John had been flown to a hospital in Khartoum, very ill with a liver abcess. The next few weeks were anxious ones but we celebrated his recovery by fixing our wedding for the following Easter, hoping to hold the service in Kabale, Uganda.

The next months were pretty hectic. John was in Omdurman –I was in Manchester. I had deputation speaking to do, driving lessons to take, medical treatment to undergo, interviews to face, visits to make, a wedding dress to sew, and a host of long-range preparations for the wedding to complete, not forgetting the necessary application for a visa. The visa was not granted.

I finally sailed for Africa in February 1964 still without a visa to enter the Sudan. I prayed that even at that late stage, the visa would come through. The thought of continued separation after our wedding was too painful to contemplate.

As we entered the Suez Canal on a hot clear shimmering day, the ship's broadcast system relayed the news. One item just numbed me where I stood. It said–all missionaries were being expelled from Southern Sudan.

The ship made its way to Mombasa. I cannot describe the sense of helplessness when there is just no means of contacting the man you have sailed thousands of miles to marry. I could only try to read his mind. He knew I was on the way out, he would surely try to stay in Africa and make contact. But Africa is a very big place. I could only cling to the hope that John was hardly likely to go back to England, and would try to contact me.

We docked at Mombasa but no one connected with the Mission had any news of John. It was the same story in Nairobi. There followed an arduous three-day overland journey to our beloved Kampala in Uganda; but something of the magic had left the air–there was no news there either. Then two days later a letter arrived at the CMS Guest House from John. He was in Khartoum and wrote: 'As far as plans are concerned, then, you should: 1. Cancel all arrangements for a wedding at Kabale. 2. Make plans for a wedding in Kampala, but make them provisional. I will try to be there! 3. Be prepared to drop everything at short notice to come here to Khartoum.' it was then exactly two weeks before our proposed wedding date!

I wasn't the only person feeling the uncertainty. Everybody around me was obviously itching to know what our plans were with a wedding day about to happen and no definite information about the bridegroom. Then came more word from John–this time by telegram. He wanted me to get a visitor's visa and go to Khartoum. This was more easily said than done but after days of questions and waiting the visa was granted.

Once again I had to pack. Packing for a long journey is a wearisome business at the best of times but when one has to include a wedding dress and cake it becomes almost bizarre. I travelled to Entebbe to arrange a flight for Khartoum. It was a Saturday which was, in fact, the day when the weekly plane from the Sudan touched down. It landed while I was at the airport. Naturally as an aeroplane landing is always fascinating I watched it touch down and taxi in. Then as the passengers came streaming out I saw the unbelievable.

John was striding across the tarmac. He had come to *me* after all!

As things can happen when mail must cover vast areas, the letter announcing his change of plans arrived three days later.

Of course the joy of our reunion after a year of separation and weeks of anxiety was tremendous. But I could see that for John there were also other emotions. In leaving Sudan he had made it highly unlikely that he could return to his post at Bishop Gwynne Theological College. He had only spent a few months there but had become convinced that it was God's place for him. For years his vision of missionary service had centred on work amongst Moslems and the Sudan seemed to be exactly the right place for him.

Even the final run up to our wedding was a chapter of accidents and mishaps. The special licence was sent to the wrong place, the Bishop who was to officiate took ill and the car was stolen and found burnt.

We even found ourselves with a flooded bedroom on the first night of our marriage!

Honeymoons end all too soon and we had to face the fact that we were jobless and homeless in the middle of Africa. We spent some time looking around and eventually found ourselves taking over from Alan and Catherine Lindsay at Buye.

There followed just under a year of service which ended with me finding myself a mother and a widow. It was a year I shall never forget: one of tremendous joy and happiness on the one hand, yet always the undercurrent of growing political tension on the other. There were still about a thousand refugees at Buye, and there was much unrest amongst them as their future remained uncertain.

John and I had our ups and downs, but who doesn't during the first year of marriage? It was such a short time, but I shall always thank God for that year with John which was so enriched as our love for and our relationship with each other grew and deepened.

2

When Dr Hindley told me that John was dead I didn't cry. Looking back now I can still see that what overcame me was not so much grief as a mixture of blind panic and unbelief. For the first time in my life I felt that the God who could allow such a tragedy to happen could not be a God of love.

I remember wanting to know where John was. I remember wanting to follow him. I wished with all my heart that I had been killed at the same time. I felt, as a person in myself, dead. I was no more than the container for a whirlpool of panic-stricken thoughts and questions, and I could not stop shaking.

Dr Hindley asked me where he could find my coat. I said it was on a peg in the corridor. He couldn't find it and returned with my nurse's cape instead saying that there were no other clothes hanging there. The reaction of surprise went in with the other strangely detached emotions–I didn't query the matter. We collected Ruth who had slept through the whole episode and drove back to the doctor's house.

I was given a sedative but I could not sleep. I lay in bed going over and over those awful moments. The men bursting in, John with the cushion, the burst of firing, John falling–it was only blood from his arm–running for help; and Dr Hindley's words. I kept longing that it would be only a dream–some nightmare–and that I could wake up to find John beside me and another normal day.

I must have slept eventually and when I awoke the morning was half passed and the funeral arrangements were well under way. I was too numb to think of a hymn when asked. After lunch the police arrived asking for me to give a description of the men who had burst in the night before.

I remember that as I began to attempt this several facts became clear in my mind. The gunman had a moustache and had been wearing a white, unusually clean raincoat. It dawned on me. He had been wearing my raincoat–yes definitely mine, the coat that was missing from the corridor peg. Then I realized that the middle man with the spear had been wearing John's raincoat and that they were masked in our scarves. These proved to be vital clues. So also did the fact that the man who told me to keep quiet, used a phrase that revealed he was not from Burundi. They were, in fact, refugees from Rwanda.

The lengthy police questioning delayed the start of the funeral service. When we finally set out for the church my mind was full of the contents of the interview and I was quite unprepared for the shock I received when we walked into the building. Hundreds of pairs of eyes met me. We walked to our pew surrounded by a charged silence broken only by the clicking sounds of sympathy from some of the women. And there in the middle of the main aisle was a plain wooden box–grotesque, hideous. My first sight of it hit me as powerfully as a physical blow. I had to keep my eyes away from it; and then the tears began to flow.

Bishop Barham took the service but my eyes were too blurred to follow and I could not take in what was going on. When it was over, students from the seminary took up the coffin and we walked out towards the burial ground. It was in no sense a cemetery, only a piece of waste ground with trees planted and a few mounds left from recent burials. John's grave had been dug alongside the small mound marking the burial place of the local pastor's child. We had stood around that sad spot only a few weeks earlier.

I was still overwhelmed with a sense of unreality. Around me was a silent crowd, vaguely recognizable as my friends. There were the usual words of scripture and as the coffin was lowered into the grave, for one brief moment I wanted to call out 'Stop'! It seemed too horribly final to lower a box into the ground and cover it with earth. Suddenly I found myself wanting some concrete proof that there was such a thing as eternal life. All my previous belief seemed empty words and I found no consolation in it all as I stood there in the burial ground.

What little consolation that I could find came from the mere existence of the people around me. I began to feel a warmth towards them all. I sensed that they knew what I was going through. I realized also that some of them were afraid that I was bitter about the Africans. I knew I had to speak to them to show that I had no bitterness for the people of Buye. I believe it was God Himself who helped me to say the few words that I did, and that I can hardly now remember.

With the burial over, we returned to Dr Hindley's house for a cup of tea. I had hardly sat down when the door burst open and the police came in frog-marching a man. I could hardly believe what I saw. They had captured John's murderer.

He fell down in front of me pleading for forgiveness; insisting that it was all a mistake, that he hadn't intended to kill, that he had never held a gun before, that he had been given too much beer to drink during the previous day and that he had never meant to do it. He sprawled there weeping and shuddering with sobs and fear. I was torn between pity for the man and anger at the whole situation. I found myself weeping bitterly and the man was taken away.

The whole business was so terribly pointless and wrong. John had not been killed by an evil murderous man, but by a weak-willed person who had never intended to kill anyone but had been bribed, filled with Dutch courage and threatened until he was another man's stooge. I truly think that the gun had been intended to frighten us and not to kill. But this made the whole thing so much worse. Why did God allow it all to happen?

For about a week after the funeral I was absolutely numb. I seemed to be an observer of life rather than a participant.

There were brief stabs of pain, but for most of the time I was living in a nightmare that was true. At times I found myself longing for death, wishing that they had killed me rather than John who was so gifted and had so much to offer.

The only ray of light in the blackness was the existence of young Ruth. Friends kept pointing out that I still had John's daughter to care for and that my life had been spared for that purpose. And yet I was becoming very angry with God. Why had He allowed this thing to happen to me? Why hadn't He intervened? Why didn't the bullets miss John as miraculously as they missed me?

One of the first decisions I had to make was whether I should take up an offer to return to England. I decided against it because I simply could not face scores of sympathetic friends and relatives, and also because I felt strangely that I shouldn't try to run away from the situation I was in. What I could see clearly, and perhaps this was one place where I managed to escape my self-centred emotions, was that some of our African friends were feeling a sense of guilt over what had been done by their fellow-tribesmen. I felt it was vital to show that I had no hard feelings. On the other hand, I needed to get away from Buye for a while.

A week after John's death, therefore, Ruth and I went to spend some time with Geoffrey and Margaret Stanley-Smith at Matana. One of the advantages of going south to Matana was that John and I had never been there so there were no memories to remind me of the past. The time at Matana proved to be one of the biggest testing periods of my life and I owe more than I shall ever realize to the patience, love and understanding of Geoffrey and Margaret.

I arrived at Matana suppressing inner resentments over God's apparent indifference and callousness. But the mood swung over the following days first into doubt and then into despair. John's burial seemed so final–how could he be in heaven? If there was a heaven, then where was it? I found no consolation or reassurance whatsoever in texts from the Bible.

On the second Sunday after arriving at the Stanley-Smith's, about thirty letters of sympathy arrived. It was a shattering but not necessarily a destructive experience. There were letters from those I had expected would write, but also letters from many others–people I had long lost contact with, from friends of John I had never seen, from Christian people I had never met and never will; letters from all over the world. They sympathized with me and of course I was soon in floods of tears. The deep unhappiness of the time swamped me. But there were other sentiments present also. Those letters assured me of many prayers and this encouraged me for I was going through a phase when I could not bring myself to pray. Some people wrote of how Christ had helped them through times of bereavement and these letters were especially helpful. I sensed then, even in my bitterness and doubting, that I was held firmly in a profoundly real band of fellowship with other Christian people.

Many African Christians came to visit me and they also brought a consolation that words of scripture at that time could not effect. Some of them were unable to put their feelings into words, but their mere presence in sad but loving silence conveyed more than words could ever express. I believe it takes courage just to sit with someone in distress, but the mere physical presence of someone who cares enough to come brings a healing power. I certainly found it so.

The immediate after-effects of the letters, however, were destructive. I was so deep in despair and hopelessness that I could no longer see any point in living. I could not pray. I could not read the Bible, and I could not accept what I had previously believed. As my unbelief grew, so the despair and panic grew also. It reached a climax on the eve of my wedding anniversary. I felt that I had reached the bottom of the pit and I dreaded the next day with its inevitable memories. If I had been able to obtain the means I would have ended my life.

And yet–as I look back now–even then I had a sense of not being alone.

That night I decided to ask Geoffrey for sleeping tablets–something to make me sleep through the day I could not face. Unfortunately he was delayed and after waiting up for a while I decided to go to bed and sit up listening for his return. I went to bed at about ten o'clock. Perhaps I dozed off...

Exactly what happened next I shall never know but I saw John again. I do not believe in spiritualism, and could never encourage anyone to seek the help of those who talk about contacting the dead. It must have been a dream or a vision. The important thing, however, was that God allowed me to experience a moment with John again, and it was a radiantly happy John who spoke to me about our daughter Ruth and the future. I shall never cease to thank God that the final memory He allowed me was of a radiant and happy John. It completely erased the memory of him dying on the bungalow floor in Buye while the Brahms' Violin Concerto played on in the background. And that dream removed my doubts about the reality of life after death.

'Our' first wedding anniversary was bearable after all. I began to experience a sense of peace. Shortly afterwards a friend reminded me of those words in the fourteenth chapter of John's Gospel: 'Peace I leave with you; my peace I give to you.' The peace Jesus called His could not have been the peace of sins forgiven for He had no need of forgiveness. My friend suggested that when Jesus used the phrase He was talking about a peace the disciples could find in the tense times they would undergo at their Master's crucifixion. If ever a group of people were to feel helpless and hopeless it was that small band of men. On the day when I also expected to feel my hopelessness and helplessness most acutely, I began to discover this peace of Christ.

I was beginning to be healed.

Three other factors brought about a complete restoration. The first was the message of Easter. I shall never experience such a 'real' Easter as that Easter 1965. Coming just over a month after John's death, the teaching of the Resurrection took on new meaning and hope. Death truly has lost its sting!

The second healing factor was little Ruth. A child only a few weeks in age is, of course, utterly dependent on its mother. As I had to see to her feeds, baths, changing, and all the paraphernalia of motherhood at that stage, it became so obvious that I was needed and that my life had a purpose. If ever I needed to be needed, it was in those first weeks after John's death.

The third factor was the news from Kabale that the preparatory school there was urgently in need of a caterer/housekeeper. I offered to do it and I received a warm welcoming letter from the staff at the school saying that their need was immediate. Again it was a case of realizing that I was genuinely needed, and needed in Africa. This meant a great deal to me at the time.

Before I could go to Kabale, however, I had to face returning to Buye to tidy up. Packing up in John's death-place couldn't but affect me. I felt anaesthetized, devoid of all feeling and I think I must have gone through all the motions rather like a robot. Friends were quick to rally round and the work was soon done.

My time at Kabale was absorbing, which was exactly what I needed. With so many children around me, often with problems of their own – both real and imagined – I had no time to dwell on my own troubles. The very business and the fact that I was needed created a healing atmosphere. As I look back now I can only see the goodness and wisdom of a Heavenly Father in it all.

As the term drew to a close it became clear that I ought to return to England for a while to visit relatives. I felt also that I was able to face them by then. We flew home in August intending to return to East Africa after a few weeks. In England, however, I began to feel that perhaps I ought to stay. Then came the news that the men who had killed John had escaped from prison. It was brought home to me that it was not safe to return and African friends wrote to me confirming this strongly.

3

The years have passed as they always do, and time heals–this can become a cliché, but it is very true. I can look back now and see a pattern of divine guidance but I cannot pretend to see it all.

I can see God's hand in leading me to an intensely satisfying post at the Church Missionary Society training college in Chislehurst. There I met good friends, and found myself working with Alan and Catherine Lindsay again. Ruth was growing up, and becoming a personality in her own right. There were several married couples in training, as well as single students, so there was always quite a number of children resident in the college, which was marvellous for Ruth. There was even a large playroom and an organized nursery group each morning, leaving me free to do my job. The post of caterer-housekeeper seemed to be tailor-made as there were comparatively few jobs I could take with my qualifications as a nurse and my responsibility as the mother of a very young child. Furthermore, being able to continue my links with CMS meant a great deal to me. It was still possible to make an indirect missionary contribution and occasionally past experience was called upon in order to advise others.

Gradually, I was able to talk and think about Africa without feeling intense pain. The fellowship within the college was a tremendous strength and a means of spiritual deepening and reassurance in my own life.

For a long time I found worship, private prayer and personal Bible study extremely difficult; God seemed very far away and unreal. This is improving gradually. I can offer no explanation or solution, but I know I must persevere.

I can see God's hand in these events, as I said before, but John's death cannot be easily fitted into the plans of a Heavenly Father who genuinely cares for His children. It would be hypocritical of me to pretend that I could see that part of the plan. Corrie Ten Boom has used an illustration that I find particularly helpful. It seems that Persian carpets are woven on great looms and the weavers work from the wrong side where everything appears to be a muddle of tangled threads and ends. It is only when one can walk round the other side of the carpet that the beautiful pattern becomes apparent. I am convinced that God is weaving a pattern with our lives, be they long or short. Even an apparently senseless murder can be seen one day as part of a pattern. For the present I can only see the tangled ends, but I am now sure that there is another side to the carpet, and that is perfect.

One lesson I have learned in all this is that Christians cannot expect to have charmed lives. One of my initial reactions to John's death was identical to that of the majority of people who face tragedy–'Why should this happen to me?' Now I can see the answer to that question is: 'Why not?' Being a Christian is not a sort of insurance policy. We must take the knocks as well and as much as anybody else. Christian happiness cannot be rooted in other people, in health or worldly fortunes. It must rest in the assurance that we have a Heavenly Father who will see that all things work together for good.

Finally, if I was to say what, on looking back, were the great healing factors in my distress I would have to say there was something intangible and something very tangible indeed. The intangible was a sense felt even in my times of blackest despair that I was not alone. Jesus never left me for one second. He was always there in the darkness, almost as real as a physical presence. Always, there was the knowledge that He had endured an even greater darkness for our sakes, and He understood and had experienced death in a way we never shall, because He has conquered death. In my suffering I caught a tiny glimpse of part of the cost of our salvation.

The tangible factor was simply people. It was the practical things that people did which made so much difference: coming to visit me even when they couldn't find words to say; writing letters especially sharing their own experiences of bereavement; offering me a job when I needed one, listening to my woes, and above all, treating me as a normal human being when I felt anything but! There was a stage when verses of Scripture became important to me too, but this was later when I was already on the way to recovery.

My greatest comfort in the blackest days was the very presence and understanding of Christ Himself, and the tremendous sense of being part of the Body of Christ, with a great awareness of the love and prayers of the dedicated Christians who stood by me. Their prayers upheld me and carried me along where alone I would have fallen, perhaps never to rise again. May God bless them all richly.

JACK WALLACE, who lives in Buckhurst Hill is married, with three children. He is a solicitor by profession, a member of Church Assembly, and active in his local church and many Christian organizations.

I

I was over forty before I noted the first mutterings of disease. Previously I had spent only two spells in hospital, both before my teens: the one with a fractured arm and the other with scarlet fever. So to someone normally robust like myself, illness appeared unthinkable.

Not long after experiencing my first symptoms I decided to visit my doctor, and he passed me on to a Harley Street surgeon. At first it seemed as if the treatment was doing the trick but after a time the symptoms returned and the surgeon sent me to a consultant physician.

It was August 1961 and I was leading a normal, active life while receiving treatment from him. In fact, that summer I was guest speaker at a house-party in Bangor, North Wales, which was the usual energetic affair. In addition to giving two daily talks, I swam, played in the finals of the tennis tournament, and climbed Snowdon. It was not surprising I was feeling a bit 'wrung-out' when I arrived home and I went to my doctor before going back to work. He insisted that I go back to the specialist but, when he heard I was taking my wife and two younger children on holiday to France the next week, he agreed to fix me up to see him on my return, perhaps because he considered my case of colitis not a particularly urgent one.

So feeling much in need of a holiday, we left London to take the car over on the cross-channel ferry and drive south. Reaching Rouen, we booked in at an hotel and went out for a late lunch. Already my symptoms were so bad that I was growing concerned.

'You just need a good rest,' my wife said, 'and you're going to have it during the next two or three weeks.'

I agreed, and the next day we pushed on to Perros Guirec, on the north coast of Brittany. It is an ideal holiday spot, with long, wide sandy beaches. It was a warm summer, and my daughter aged fourteen and my younger son aged twelve, were in and out of the sea the whole time, enjoying themselves tremendously. I was determined that having planned a family holiday I was not going to abandon it without good reason.

But every day, and particularly each night, I was getting worse. On our first Sunday morning we went to morning service in the little Protestant 'Temple' and heard of Jesus Christ, 'Le même hier, aujourd'hui et toujours'. By the next Sunday I had to drag myself to the service having stuck out the week in the hope of improvement. Imagine my horror when I found my suit that I hadn't worn for seven days hanging on me like a sack. But still hardly able to believe the evidence, and being of a somewhat mule-headed turn of mind, I counteracted my wife's suggestion that we fly home. By the following Sunday I was conducting morning prayer from my bed! Soon I had given in and we were on our way home.

It took us two days to get back to the Channel–a truly nightmare-like drive for my wife. We stayed overnight at Avranches and Rouen to break the journey, and I managed to perk up sufficiently to entertain a young French boy from the Bangor house-party at Rouen. When we boarded the ferry the Purser was good enough to let me have his bunk.

We were due to pick up our eldest son at Gatwick later that afternoon on his return from six months in Mombasa. My wife had to telephone my sister and make arrangements for someone to meet him, and we made straight for home. There was little trace of holiday spirits when we finally reached it, and never have I been more grateful to fall flat into my own bed.

My consultant kindly broke into his week-end golf to come and see me and made arrangements for me to go without delay into hospital. I little realized that I was to remain there for over six months off and on.

I was to receive devoted medical care and attention throughout my stay in hospital to which I undoubtedly owe my life. Nobody really knows the causes of my complaint, ulcerative colitis, although there are many theories about it. Some trace it to a physical cause such as a virus; others to a deep-seated psychological or nervous cause. If ever the cause is discovered it will be through the efforts of dedicated people such as cared for and treated me during my illness.

Dr Brian Webster, who, though not in charge of my case, used to visit me, and give me encouragement explained how, in response to drugs, some of us are 'quick ovens' and some 'slow'. Sad to say, I seemed to be the latter for after four weeks in hospital, the X-rays revealed that the drugs were not having the desired effect.

Meanwhile despite blood transfusions, I was becoming weaker and weaker. I am grateful for the many pints of blood from unknown donors that I benefited from in the weeks that followed, for surgery was now essential.

With most people details of illnesses are of no particular interest unless and until they become fellow-sufferers, so I won't dwell on too much detail. I know that I signed my consent in October 1961 for a colectomy and an ileostomy, then three months later for an abdomino-perineal resection. A rudimentary medical explanation had been given me about each, but I was pretty doubtful even as to the spellings let alone what they meant!

It was clear, however, that the first operation was in time only by a very few hours, as the main organ concerned had burst. I came out of the anaesthetic grumbling to my wife that they were very slow, and I was still waiting to have the operation. She assured me that I had had it and I rapidly discovered how right she was! I certainly would not volunteer to go through the next few hours again. My wife sat with me much of the time reading verses from the Bible and it is impossible in mere words to express the reality of Christ's presence then and on many later crisis points in my illness. He granted me a realization of Himself, neither visible or audible, which, odd though it seems, I have not apprehended in my ordinary everyday experience.

Apart from my two major trips to the theatre, I had one other small visit and a couple of general anaesthetics for dressings. On every occasion, whether being trundled on the trolley to the lift or waiting for the anaesthetist I had the wonderful assurance that the Lord was my Shepherd and though I walked in the 'Valley of the Shadow of Death' He really was with me.

When I was recovering from my first encounter with the surgeon I had to learn to walk again. This was done with the aid of a four-wheeled iron contraption. After doing some twenty paces, and feeling as if I had cracked the three-minute mile, I collapsed into a chair. I was reading the novel, *Exodus,* at the time, and picking it up I opened it at my place to read the chapter heading: 'They that wait upon the Lord shall renew their strength...' At that stage, weak as a kitten, I wasn't concerned 'to run and not be weary', but I was anxious 'to walk and not faint' as the verse continues. I gladly accepted God's assurance that I would eventually do so.

During my illness, pain and the thought of death had to be faced. My wife says that at one stage, she had to bring herself to abandon all her claims on me in utter resignation to God's will. But she then received a series of wonderful promises from God as she read John chapters 14, 15 and 16. These were summed up in the words, 'If ye shall ask anything in my name, I will do it' (John 14.14). This enabled her to face the pessimism of the doctors and surgeons when they kept insisting, 'We're not over the hump yet'. And with confidence based on God's word she overcame her natural reticence and told them that, as I was the subject of many prayers, I was going to recover!

My wife brought me many texts while I was 'inside'–as well as a bit of extra supper to supplement what the authorities provided! At first she would quote verses like Philippians 4.13: 'I can do all things through Christ', but I insisted that as I could not be bothered to *do* anything, I only wanted to know what God could do for me. So after that she brought me verses mainly from the Psalms, and I learned to love particularly Psalm 27.14 (RSV) 'Wait for the Lord; be strong, and let your heart take courage; yea, wait for the Lord!'

Illness naturally brought a complete disinterest in outside affairs and I just could not bother about my office work. God wonderfully overruled here, and provided a more than adequate replacement throughout my enforced absence. But after nearly ten months away it was with some dread that I got ready to return to work. On the first Monday morning, at the top of the personal column in *The Times* was the promise 'As thy days so shall thy strength be' (Deuteronomy 33.25). Next day, despite that encouragement I was naturally a bit tired and wondered if I should not take a little time off. There, in the verse for that day was the direct instruction, 'Arise, and go on into the city, and it shall be told thee what thou must do' (Acts 9.6). I always imagine the Lord with a real twinkle in His eye! And His promises stood me in good stead.

Having outlined the main course of my illness I want to go

back and comment on particular lessons learnt, for during those months I had time to reflect on many things.

Just getting used to being in hospital was a lesson in itself, when you are usually active and have suddenly to throw everything up and lie in bed. It was salutary to realize that though we affirm our belief in 'justification by faith', God has to teach us again and again that it is truly 'by grace are ye saved through faith...it is the gift of God...*not of works* lest any man should boast' (Ephesians 2.8–10). Unfortunately what we sometimes think of as progress in the Christian life consists in multiplying activity after frenzied activity.

I became aware, during the weeks of enforced idleness, that Christ cared as much for me whether I was ill and inactive or cramming my life full with Christian busy-ness. It is always good to realize that we are dispensable, and that both the Church and the world can survive perfectly well after our removal at the drop of a hat!

Furthermore, the great lesson I began to learn in hospital was that Jesus, 'though he were a Son, yet learned he obedience by the things which he suffered' (Hebrews 5.7–8). God's only begotten Son delighted to do His Father's will, yet in a sense His sufferings taught Him true obedience. His innate ability to obey was tested to the uttermost, brought to maturity and demonstrated to the world at Gethsemane and Calvary, in His sufferings. So, in a much lesser degree I, too, was learning obedience.

Most of the patients in the public ward I was in were inarticulate on any subject save that of their own disease and its symptoms! If you were a sufferer anxious to regale another with detailed descriptions of your ailment you usually found them faintly interested and waiting only to counter-attack with their own experiences.

But there are, through Christ, other more positive aspects of suffering we can talk about. As a Christian I felt that I could relate pain to Christ's redemptive activity in us, seeing His purpose fulfilled as we are strengthened in the Holy Spirit, and renewed in fellowship with our heavenly Father.

I like to think that this witness was unobtrusive. One of the first conversations of a spiritual nature I had in hospital was with a Jewish patient much concerned about his health. He came over to show me a book of Hebrew prayers and asked what I thought of it, as 'he knew I was a religious man'. I'm not sure how he knew, but in a ward one is never unobserved, and no doubt he may have noticed me reading the Bible, or quietly praying. Since I could only pray lying down and didn't move my lips like Hannah, I doubt if it was the latter! The fact is, that if we love the Lord, it seems to show.

I had other spiritual conversations and one or two short chats with Christian nurses, I say 'short' deliberately, because I knew the nurse had a job to do and much as she might like to talk of Christ, it was wrong to keep her hanging about my bed for longer than necessary when there were always other men requiring her attention. On occasions I lent a couple of these nurses Bible commentaries which they found helpful.

But many of the nurses were not Christians and were suspicious of 'Bible punchers'. I gained the confidence of one of these by getting my legal partner to chase up the belongings of one of her favourite patients. He was a simple minded man who was having trouble under the Rent Acts. All I had to do was to mention the need and leave the necessary work to my willing colleague, but as so often happens, the doing of some comparatively minor chore broke down the barriers.

I found that as a patient I could often be more helpful to other patients than an outsider. This made me think hard about the role of hospital visitors, however well-intentioned. Daily, into the wards full of pallid, self-centred patients there was injected a swarm of various visitors, that is always assuming that they did not fetch up in the wrong ward, lost in the Cretan labyrinth of corridors stretching out from the entrance hall. But having arrived, with what motives did they come visiting? It is not good enough to say, 'I simply must see poor old so-and-so'. When I was 'poor old so-and-so' I was conscious at times of being a target for pet ideas, an unwilling victim exposed to sermonizing, while under mental and physical disadvantages.

Truth so often lies more in a relationship than in mere words. Job's comforters started off with the right idea: 'they sat with him on the ground seven days and seven nights, and no one spoke a word to him, for they saw that his suffering was very great' (Job 2.13 RSV). The grip of a loving hand can mean so much more than a well-meant homily.

Eager 'do-gooders', flanked by choirs and determined to preach the gospel in great detail, tend to forget that pain is physically and mentally exhausting, and at times just downright boring. The average patient just cannot take much, and if he cannot see the speaker or singer without getting a crick in his neck or a corkscrew spine, he just will not want to know more.

More often, instead of listening to his visitor, a weary or depressed patient needs a sympathetic listener who seems to understand his need, to find relief from his sense of loneliness or failure. For just over six months, my world consisted solely of Ward C4, and the visitors who helped me most were content on the whole to be reasonably quiet and listen, with real (or feigned?) interest to the no doubt boring details I wished to communicate.

And then there are the hospital chaplains. It is a great shame that so many fail to realize the unique position of privilege and responsibility they hold. There are plenty of people to chirrup to the patient, 'How are you, dear?' People in hospital expect the chaplain to go a bit further and speak straightforwardly of Jesus Christ. Many a person without admitting it, is anxiously waiting a word of comfort from the Lord. Maybe the patient is feeling guilty at this utter human dependence on the ministrations of others, or is finding it hard to believe that his body is simply letting him down. How tragic that so often the hungry anxious 'sheep' look up and are not fed by the 'shepherd'. Although I used to receive the Sacrament at the hands of the Padre in hospital pretty regularly, more to encourage him than anything else, sad to say I found him unwilling to talk personally about Jesus Christ.

In fact, I got more help from another visitor, the wife of another patient, than from the Padre. Of the many words of encouragement from the Lord that she gave me I remember especially this from Bishop Moule:

> 'The Lovers of the Lord are indeed unable to explain, to themselves or others, how this concurrence of "All things" works out its infallible issues in them. And the observer from without cannot understand their certainty that it is so. But the fact is there, given and assured, not by speculation upon events, but by personal knowledge of an Eternal Person.'

I copied this thought into a book on prayer by H. E. Fosdick that she also gave me and which I found a real practical help.

Another helpful visitor was the Rev. David Sheppard (now the Bishop of Woolwich, then Warden of the Mayflower Family

Centre). During a visit I was able to tell him about one of my fellow-patients, Charlie, an ex-commando Regimental Sergeant Major. Charlie had been to Bible Class at St Mary's Church, Islington, where David Sheppard had been a curate. I had had one or two talks with Charlie about the Lord and told David this. Within minutes of approaching his bed, David was talking directly to him and his wife of the Good Shepherd who knew His sheep. They were in great need at the time and listened gratefully. Before we eventually parted, Charlie told me he had so much to be thankful for that he was now praying or 'putting his hands together' as he called it, every night.

Some months after leaving hospital it was good to see Charlie again, and at the same time another patient, Jack. He was a commercial traveller, who had suffered from the same disease for twenty years. Like me he went down to theatre trusting the words of Psalm 23 and confident in the prayers of members of his church, a small nearby mission. We were very worried about him for he lay after the operation at death's door for many days, but God brought him through and answered prayer.

2

Another subject that exercised me in hospital was prayer. I found it a great privilege and opportunity to pray from time to time for fellow patients like Charlie and Jack. 'From time to time' is important because there is a lot of nonsense talked by some Christians about being 'laid aside' by illness in order to concentrate on prayer for the needs of mankind. We are laid aside in order to get better, and usually we are too weak to do more than merely 'turn our eyes upon Jesus'. Healthy Christians must be careful not to give their brethren who are sick, guilt complexes over this.

As it was, there were times when I could pray for others in our ward. One of these was George, who had suffered an unidentified stomach pain for years and his surgeon's explorations had been in vain. On the day he was due for a final attempt to find the cause in theatre, I told him I was praying specifically for him, claiming the promise 'Hitherto you have asked nothing in my name; ask, and you will receive, that your joy may be full' (John 16.24 RSV).

On George's return from theatre, the nurse put a little bottle on his bedside table. It contained a dirty, greyish plum stone which had been stuck in his gut for years! That evening I shared the good news with the group of men at our end of the ward, and we talked of how Christ answers our prayers offered in faith, no matter how feeble. I pointed out that, whatever view they took, George's joy was certainly 'full', in accord with the Lord's promise. George was certainly impressed, and accepted a copy of *Beginning with Christ* (The Navigators). Even if a little embarrassed, I always found men glad to know someone was praying for them before an operation, and usually ready to accept and read a booklet such as *Words of Comfort* (Scripture Gift Mission).

Then there was an Irishman in the ward, whose long dressing-gown used to sweep the floor. For twenty-odd years, Pat had put off telling his doctor of the pain he was enduring. I found out he was a Baptist, but had backslidden since coming to England. When he was told the date of his operation, he came over to my bed, oozing apprehension from every pore. I at once invited him to bow his head with me and, in a brief prayer, we committed him to the mercy of God. He gladly joined in, then told me had had come over specifically to ask for my prayers.

Prayer wrung from anguished hearts, is none the less real for being self-centred. It is good to be reminded that, in times of trial, Bible prayers are mainly self-orientated. Look at Jacob, for instance, praying as Esau approaches with four hundred men, 'Deliver me...for I fear him' (Genesis 32.11). Look at the Psalms and look at our Lord, as he offers up 'prayers and supplications with tears' in Gethsemane, and in the great cry of dereliction on the cross, 'Why hast thou forsaken me?'

There are some who suggest it is even wrong for Christians to cry out in pain, But this is a Stoic philosophy, appropriate perhaps to Islam, but not to Jesus Christ. We are called to offer and present ourselves, our souls and bodies as a reasonable, holy and living sacrifice to God. Surely then we can ask God to use our pain, turning it into sacrificial prayer and praise, in the furtherance of His holy will for His great plan of redemption?

I think, for example, of a sick woman in bed for her entire life and often in pain, who offered up her sufferings to God in such a way, beseeching Him to use it in bringing into being a place for others similarly afflicted. She has now gone to be with Christ, but the object of her prayer is now complete. Seeing St Christopher's Hospice,* towering over Lawrie Park Road,

* In fact St Christopher's Hospice was built in 1967, entirely by gifts. It is a new religious and medical foundation caring for those in pain and suffering due to advanced cancer or other long-term illness. It aims to show the love of God for them in skilled nursing and medical care, in the use of every scientific means of relieving distress, and by providing understanding with personal sympathy in a community planned for them where they can stay as long as they need this help. It is becoming a centre for research and teaching in the many and varied aspects of such illness, including its impact upon the families concerned.

Although the Regional Hospital Board help towards the maintenance of approximately half of the patients, other grants and gifts are always needed to meet the balance of maintenance for no patient is ever refused on financial grounds.

Sydenham, we can surely realize the intercessory power of her sacrificial offering of her pain 'for His body's sake–the Church'.

As a member of 'the body of Christ' I certainly learned new lessons in hospital of what being 'in Christ' means. In moments of weakness, I began to appreciate the 'communion of saints' more fully, as I relied on the persistent and prevailing prayers of my friends, other members of the one body. My wife used to tell me of the number of folk praying for me, and it humbled me to tears at times. She hinted that I was doing more for the kingdom of God lying there in bed, than in previous years of tearing all over the place!

I was reminded forcibly in hospital how useless it is to imagine we can start turning to Christ when things begin to go wrong. Generally it will be too late, and desperate sickness seems to lead as much to loneliness of heart as to conversion. But if God's Word is already precious and planted in the heart, how graciously the Holy Spirit brings it to remembrance. The Bible became more precious to me in hospital than ever before, and I was grateful I had memorized parts of it from time to time.

For example, on the day the Registrar warned me of the strong possibility of my having to undergo surgery, God reminded me of Acts 2.25–26, 'I foresaw the Lord always before my face, for he is on my right hand, that I should not be moved. Therefore did my heart rejoice and my tongue was glad...'

The night before my first operation, while a couple of medical students were helping the houseman fix me up, a barrister friend of mine arrived, much too late for visiting but he was allowed to pass on to me a verse. Psalm 50.15 was his choice from that morning's *Daily Light*: 'Call upon me in the day of trouble: I will deliver thee, and thou shalt glorify me.' This same friend some months later came in again after visiting at the end of one of my most dismal days. He took my hand and simply said, 'Hitherto has the Lord helped us. Henceforth unto Him. Hallelujah!' This it transpired was his sermon outline for the following Sunday. I can say that even if his congregation did not benefit, it certainly bucked me up.

I was aware in the ward that there were men around me who did not have the Word of God in their hearts, and the Bible requires us all to be living letters known and read of all men. I remember the arguments I had with another patient who was an atheist. I refuted him in public with arguments from the

Scriptures not so much to do him any good, but to counteract the potential harm he might have caused. When we were alone, doing our dressings in the bathroom, he used to pour out some of his woes to me for he was an unhappy person.

Then there was the Roman Catholic who gave me a medallion of the Virgin Mary, to which he seemed to ascribe certain magical powers. He knew well my views on this subject, but I took it in the spirit in which he gave it. I felt to do otherwise would have been churlish, and surely would not have commended the Saviour, who graciously received from men what was offered Him in sincerity.

But there were others who had nothing to give or receive. I remember vividly a man of about sixty who had to be operated on for cancer of the throat. He had not been told it was cancer but I think he suspected. On the morning of his operation, he burst into tears as the sister came round and she did her best, but she had nothing very deep to pass on. Sadly the man never came out of the anaesthetic.

Yet there were medical staff who offered spiritual as well as medical help. I received much encouragement from fellowship with Dr Brian Webster. His grasp of his healing vocation and his conversation brought me spiritual and mental aid during tense and difficult moments. This sense of Christian vocation in all healing is something that Dr William Barclay has written about:

> 'The surgeon with his new techniques and miracle drugs can now effect the most amazing cures –whether he knows it or not, Jesus says to him through His Spirit, "These people must be helped and healed. You must do it." '

The saint's names of many of our hospitals remind us that their origins lie deep in Christian charity; whether the human agents are conscious of His presence or not, the work of healing, care and compassion is always Christ's. Man's need is the meeting-point for Christian or non-Christian medical staff. John Taylor points this out in one of his Newsletters for the Church Missionary Society:

> 'Perhaps the most significant task of medical workers in the service of the Gospel today lies in the dialogue which they can develop in the course of their work with their fellow-practitioners who do not share their faith. And the main topic for such

dialogue must surely be the nature of man –the man whom they are seeking to heal. Has his physical breakdown necessarily made him less of a man? Or is it part of his search for self-knowledge, or a vicarious bearing of the sin of society? Does the doctor recognize that he may often bring that man the health which means inner integrity even when he cannot bring him the healing of his sickness? In the process of eliminating pain, does he take care to ensure that the pain, while it lasts, shall not be suffered in vain? And if death must come, does he see it as his responsibility not merely to sedate but to help his patient to meet death?'

Surely there could be much closer co-operation between ministers and doctors, demonstrating a concern for our human unity-in-trinity of body, mind and spirit? We thank God for our food and hold Harvest Thanksgiving Services, recognizing that all our sustenance comes from Him. We might similarly recognize Him as the source of all healing, perhaps by establishing it as a custom that everyone about to have a serious operation could have a visit from the hospital chaplain. For Christians, a service of Holy Communion could be arranged for the laying-on of hands or anointing with oil. This is not to say it would be right to suggest to any patient, reconciled to a major operation as God's will, that all he needs for his healing is the laying-on of hands and anointing with oil. Such a suggestion may upset him, causing him to fear that he may be limiting God's power by relying on the surgeon's knife at all. We cannot prescribe to God how He is to make men whole, but there is a place for all these things.

I attended a service of laying-on of hands at Burrswood, the late Dorothy Kerin's Home of Healing at Groombridge. There I met a minister to whom God had granted a remission of myeloma when he was past all medical hope, after a bishop had anointed him within the framework of Holy Communion. Although he died some months later, his widow testifies to the great joy and uplift God gave them, and others through them, during that precious period of remitted health.

When I look back on my experience of pain, I smile to remember only a few months before it I read Brian Hession's book *Determined to Live* about his fight with cancer, and felt quite sure that I could never put up with anything like that myself! But at the time of our suffering God does not always reveal what fruitfulness in us He has in mind. Shortly before I left hospital for the last time my surgeon explained to a colleague as they talked over my bed, 'This fellow has no right to be here'. He was quite correct for none of us is alive at all but by God's grace, and He loves us in spite of our cowardice, lack of faith and disobedience, and continually seeks to produce in us that quality of obedience that Christ Jesus had to learn. But because of this, when we are plunged into the sea of suffering, we have a Pilot with a personal experience of every rock, headland, shoal and quicksand we encounter.

I was reminded by a friend in a letter how our sufferings can be the gateway to new opportunities for service. It was when I was at home between operations that the letter came in which he said,

> 'The one purpose of the branch is to bear fruit (John 15). And the fruit-bearing branch comes in for special attention by the Husbandman (our heavenly Father). When we are fulfilling His purpose and bringing forth fruit, His bright design is that we should bring forth more fruit, for it is only as we bear more fruit that we glorify Him (verse 8). But before we can produce more fruit, it is necessary for the divine Husbandman to prune the branch (verse 2), and this seemed to me to be (from the Godward side) the explanation of all you have been through since last August. It is the Father's pruning knife used with all the skill and wisdom of His unerring love to bring forth in you yet more precious fruit. From your own knowledge you will recall how vitally necessary it is for the vine to be cut back, and, as we think, cut back ruthlessly until it would seem to the ignorant to be quite ruined. I remember so vividly seeing all this being done to the vines on the hill terraces when I was a chaplain in Italy –it almost seemed as though there was nothing left but a mere stump. But later –what a change. First the new shoots, then the branches, then the rich clusters.'

My subsequent experience revealed the correctness of my friend's judgment, for slowly my horizons have widened through my experience of pain. One direct result in my opinion, was my meeting Leslie Kingston who, against tremendous human odds, had set himself the task of providing homes for aged sufferers with ileostomies, many of whom have practical problems needing intimate and sympathetic help. Through the Christian Teamwork Institute of Education (now the Grubb Institute), the Kingston Trust has been linked up with the

Abbeyfield Society and homes are being opened on the Abbeyfield pattern. My existing interest in Dr Cicely Saunders' work among cancer patients has vastly increased, and it has been a great joy to see God bringing St Christopher's Hospice into existence. Then I have become closely involved in such projects as the work among meths drinkers at Spitalfields Crypt, and the Christian Hospital at Ghorveh in Kurdistan.

On a more personal note, it was delightful to have two of my friends from the ward, Charlie and Jack, come with their wives to hear Dr Cicely Saunders speak at a meeting in our house in the autumn of 1962.

'Suffering trains us to endure, and endurance brings proof that we have stood the test, and this proof is the ground of hope' (Romans 5.4 NEB). Certainly an ileostomy keeps one in touch with the basic fact of our breath-by-breath mortality, and increases one's concern for all sufferers. George Matheson, the blind Scottish preacher summed it up for me when he wrote,

> 'My God, I have never thanked Thee for my thorn. I have thanked Thee for my roses, but not once for my thorn...Show me that I have climbed to Thee by the path of pain. Show me that my tears have made my rainbows. Those miserable, prickly thorns! What eternal weights of glory they may be.'

now you may like to read . . .

Two booklets

Depression—A Christian's Experience
price 7½p
A first-hand explanation of the illness by a sufferer who has also been a nurse—relating especially to the special problems of the Christian.

Letter from a Surgeon, by S. Farrant Russell
price 5p
A friendly and informal 'letter to a patient in hospital' designed to make hospital life seem less bewildering, and to offer some Christian thinking on life and suffering at a time when there may be opportunities for reflection.

And a book

Church and Hospital, Margaret Welch
price 25p
A practical book setting out how a hospital works and suggesting how Christians can best help in their visiting, ward services, etc.

. . . further Falcon titles